Hitchhiking into Recovery

A JOURNEY OF CONNECTION, HEALING, AND HOPE

THE BEAUTIFUL UGLY LESSONS SERIES

PAULA ROBBINS

Edited by Melissa Rudder
Cover Design by Kristina Edstrom
Author Photo by Ari Hunniford

An Imprint for GracePoint Publishing (www.GracePointPublishing.com)
GracePoint Matrix, LLC
624 S. Cascade Ave, Suite 201
Colorado Springs, CO 80903
www.GracePointMatrix.com
Email: Admin@GracePointMatrix.com

EMP⊙WER
P   R   E   S   S

SAN # 991-6032

A Library of Congress Control Number has been requested and is pending.
ISBN: (Paperback) 978-1-966346-40-1
eISBN: 978-1-966346-60-9

Books may be purchased for educational, business, or sales promotional use.
For distribution queries contact Sales@IPGbook.com
For non-retail bulk order requests contact Orders@GracePointPublishing.com

Printed in U.S.A

DEDICATION

To every alcoholic or addict who has wondered if they would ever get their act together and keep just one damn promise to themselves or anyone they loved.

To my grandmother.

To my beautiful daughters, Angel and Rae.

To all my friends and family who have stood by me through many ups and downs, ever supporting my love for life and healing.

CONTENT WARNING

This book contains descriptions of child and domestic abuse, child neglect, sexual abuse, drug and alcohol use, a suicide attempt, and other traumatic events that may be disturbing to the reader.

TABLE OF CONTENTS

Notes from the Author

Terminology: There are many ways to name substance abuse, addiction, severe alcohol and drug use, and even the ICD-10 (International Classification of Diseases, 10th ed.) code of substance abuse disorder. Regardless of the terminology you prefer, I hope you will read beyond its phrasing, knowing that the intention is to focus on the path of solution to seemingly hopeless states of mind and body.

Names: Many of the names used in the stories are of the actual individuals I'm writing about. Some are pseudonyms, changed to protect their anonymity.

Trigger warning: Some of the stories I share may trigger feelings about your own history of child abuse, neglect, abandonment, or perhaps your own history with addiction, alcoholism, or a rough moment in recovery. While I've done a great deal of healing work within the twelve steps, through psychology and psychiatry, energy healing, metaphysics, hypnotherapy, and a few shamans, I was triggered a bit when writing it, too!

INTRODUCTION

The Four Pillars of Connection

IT WAS FEBRUARY 1988 when I (almost) accidentally began a journey into a life that was far beyond my imagination at that time. I was in the throes of addiction and alcoholism and deeply wounded by many forms of trauma and abuse. I had ideals in my mind of the life I wanted to live and the chains of familial lineage I wanted to break, yet I couldn't wait to take the next drink or drug to escape the cycle of self-sabotage, shame, anger, neglect, and pure bewilderment.

As you read this introduction, perhaps you or someone you care about has faced a similar battle. I would guess you agree that addiction, in any form, is a prevalent issue in the world.

Being in recovery from severe substance abuse since 1988, I have been fascinated by the many paths to recovery that are available and why I stayed in recovery when others may not have. My curiosity and openness to the resources that help individuals with recovery have been vast. I've explored various research from religious affiliation to trauma healing and from exercise programs to plant medicine. My interest in the paths that others have taken successfully has shown me that what lights up one soul and helps them to heal and live a healthy life in recovery may not be as effective for another.

However, one of the common threads to all paths of successful recovery I have found in my fascination with the subject is the depth of connection the individual feels once they are on a successful healing journey. This has actually been put to scientific study and cultural experimentation as well.

A favorite study, titled Rat Park, by Bruce K. Alexander, Professor Emeritus, Simon Fraser University, 1978, was conducted to determine if addiction is physical or emotional. The gist of the study was that rats were placed in isolation cages with two drink options: water and morphine-sweetened water. While in isolation, the rats tended to drink the morphine water almost exclusively. When they moved the individual rats that had been in isolation to the larger community with numerous rats in the same "park," the rats that had been isolated avoided the drugged water and drank predominantly the plain water.

The study set out to prove that one of the primary solutions to severe alcohol or drug abuse is, yes, connection. Once the rats had a place to socialize, play, and connect with other rats, they were less interested in being physically altered by the effects of the morphine.

The importance of connection to others, to your divinity, and to a purpose is deeply beneficial and transformative on any healing path, especially the path of recovery.

This is the core message of this entire book.

Connection is the foundation that builds the house to not only recovery from addiction or alcoholism, but to healing in general.

This book is written in two parts. In Part I, I share my own personal stories of disconnect and how I came to a humble admission of my alcoholism and addiction, and in Part II, I share how I began my life of connection and recovery. I detail the primary roots of my own disconnect and the power of connection that has been so remarkable.

I share some details that are vulnerable, raw, and ultimately transformative to my own walk. These are real stories of abuse, dysfunction, and heartbreak that later became redemption, hope, and healing to a degree that I truly could have never imagined possible.

Much of what I share relates to my experience in the twelve-step programs. While I am accepting and supportive of truly *any* path that helps someone to heal and live a life of their highest potential, the foundation of my healing journey lies in the connection to the people, my own spirit, and my life's purpose because of my involvement with the twelve-step programs and the principles I have learned and practice actively.

One of these many principles is unity.

With the intention of unifying to support recovery and healing, I hope that regardless of your thoughts or opinions on any route to recovery, I offer you a perspective on the power that connection brings to the healing path of addiction and many other ailments of the soul.

Just above, I mentioned that connection is the foundation that supports the house to not only recovery from addiction or alcoholism, but to all healing. Let's explore an analogy of a well-built home. Imagine a concrete foundation and four solid pillars, one in each corner of the foundation, which make for the basis of a solid and secure structure. Once these aspects are in place, no matter what is added for framing, siding, a roof, or furnishings, the foundation is strong, secure, and stabilized to endure the bad weather of life over a long period of time.

Over the course of these many decades in recovery, I have found that there are four pillars of connection that have been the foundational guideposts to successful recovery in my own life and the lives of those I respect the most, those with whom I have shared the journey. In Part II of the book, I reveal how I came to align with the pillars and how each one clarified itself in my life.

In my personal walk of life, these are not multiple choice; they are all of the above, and truly what has offered structure, warmth, and sanctuary, even in the darkest and most disconnected of times. These pillars are more than a key to a solid structure, too. They are the insurance policy that keeps my "home" and spirit secure during the storms of life.

Before I outline the pillars in greater detail, I would like to touch on the meaning of the word *spiritual*. For some, it is closely aligned with the word *religion*. And while I feel that there is nothing wrong with someone having love for their religion, spirituality and religion are not the same thing.

When we think about the human spirit or the spirit of someone we love, we don't automatically assign any sect, doctrine, or belief system. The same applies when we think of the spirit of kindness, love, or even laughter. We consider the essence.

The essence or energy of each pillar truly has its own spirit. Please keep an open mind as you read them. Better yet, I encourage you to embrace the culmination of all four pillars in your own life. Consider the places you could thrive if you were part of a relatable spiritual community, valued for your contribution in service, deeply impacted by a wise mentor, and grounded with love through daily connection with your own divinity. I genuinely feel that if you do, your spiritual foundation and inherent wisdom will become more enriched, enlightened, and evolved.

The Four Pillars of Connection

Spiritual Community

Community is about being like-minded and having common interests, actions, and goals. When you are in community with like-minded friends who are also abusing substances or are in active addiction, there is a sense of community. However, it is altered by the mere nature of how substances affect your intellect, emotions, and even your spirit. This is often still very isolating and disconnecting as you are abusing substances. In your heart of hearts, you know something isn't right with your soul. The connection to others in this sense is more about justification because "you aren't the only one," rather than a true sense of a connected community with a spiritual foundation that offers integrity.

However, when people unite for a common good, such as recovery, spirituality, or supporting one another to simply live better, the connection that the community provides has a deeper meaning. The clarity of mind and heart is pure.

Of course, finding a community that feels aligned with your own soul is key. This is where you need to dig with courage, willingness, and an open mind to clarify what you stand for and what you also need support with.

The twelve-step communities have supported my path and have stood for hope, offering a safe, forgiving, and educational environment. Others may resonate better with a religious community, a wellness or fitness community, a service to humanity collaborative, or any number of communities that have the right *spirit* to serve the soul's purpose and inherent need to evolve. If the community you are considering shines with a spirit that lights you up, I would call that *spiritual* by the foundational meaning of the word.

Service from Your Spirit

You may wonder how giving your time and energy to others fosters connection.

Let me count the ways...

One of the profound benefits of the service work I've experienced is the light it has shed on my own challenges and struggles. At times, it was beneficial simply because I took a break from my own difficulties, allowing me to reset emotionally and mentally. Other times, it offered me a different perspective that was deeply needed.

The act of contributing to the lives of others creates a great deal of purpose, reward, satisfaction, and fulfillment. Just knowing that something you said or did enhanced the life of someone else can be very connecting. It allows your spirit to serve in a way that enriches both others and you.

Finding a way to serve that is meaningful to you is where it becomes easy, natural, and deeply connecting. This may be serving close loved ones who need your engagement and presence. This may mean volunteering for a cause that calls to you. This may be more personal, such as becoming a mentor. Regardless of your choice for offering your time and energy, with selflessness, humility, and commitment, it will enrich your life and deepen your connection to your spirit. This is a promise.

Of course, giving of your time also raises the topic of balance. I'm sure you've heard the saying that you cannot pour from an empty cup. While this is very true, and managing time is a factor to consider with sincerity, I can assure you that once your heart heeds the call, the reward and fulfillment of offering your love through service is among the things that fill this proverbial cup.

Spiritual Mentor

The role of a mentor is to guide you on a path they have already walked. In twelve-step communities, a mentor is often referred to as a sponsor. I think these are interchangeable, but to clarify, a mentor is someone who offers guidance and per- haps a road map, while a sponsor is someone who both guides the way and walks beside you on the road. They possess wis- dom gained from their experiences of overcoming many challenges and obstacles that you may just be beginning to face. Additionally, you have chosen them with humility, having inten- tionally asked them to guide you. Humility and vulnerability go hand in hand, and by the very nature of vulnerability, you allow for a deeper connection to this one soul. Mentorship appears in various ways when you are part of a community. While I en- courage you to form relationships with those known for their wisdom or experience, I more strongly encourage you to iden- tify a single individual with whom you will nurture a deeper relationship and to communicate clearly with them about your desire to receive mentorship or sponsorship. The intention is to gain what they already have—wisdom, knowledge, skills, or even demeanor—by learning what they've learned or doing what they've done.

Daily Divine Alignment

The practice of daily alignment with the Divine has been the single most life-changing practice I have ever committed to. This is a practice that had been presented to me numerous times throughout my early years in recovery, but one that I didn't fully commit to until 2001. The practice is to dedicate a quiet time each day to prayer or meditation, inviting unity and alignment with Divinity into your body, mind, and spirit. It is about aligning your given free will with the will of the Divine and setting the foundation of your day upon this alignment and intention. The central premise of this alignment is the principle of trust that the Divine truly wants what is best for you. When you align your free will with Divine Will, your actions, words, instincts, and responses are more spiritually guided.

Through my own efforts with a sustainable daily ritual, I have experienced noticeable shifts in how my day unfolds. The most prevalent of these shifts is responding to life's situations rather than reacting to them. When I make the time to set the foundation of my day with divine alignment and surrender, I feel supported, more intuitive, and generally more trusting of the Great Mystery. There are divine principles that naturally flow in the day to include trust, unity, brotherhood, sisterhood, humility, integrity, and often, joy.

The four pillars provide connection in a way that is profound and thorough, enabling a rich and meaningful life. These four magical pillars of connection are the foundation of my life today. They are the "chain breakers" and the gifts that breathe life into my soul.

I hope that you read this book with an open mind and open heart. The solution that I am presenting has shaped my life in a sound, stable, and often joyful experience of living and thriving that would feel quite the opposite if I didn't have it in full form and practice.

I speak from experience here.

If there's anything I know, it's that we all want to be peaceful, happy, and secure. When we have self-love and continue to seek peace, happiness, and security for ourselves, we can reach back in time to moments when we were anything but, and it may sting a little. This is part of the healing process that I've undergone. As I wrote these stories, I laughed, cried, and experienced moments of great shame and redemption—sometimes all in one paragraph. The emotions, the stories, and the lessons are all a part of the path that led to sharing this with you.

Some of the moments and periods of time shared are truly awful. All of them reveal their beauty as they come full circle, at least to me. Some of the value is easy to identify as having been learned the hard way. Some was a sly gift from the Divine that I would have never acknowledged had I not kept going.

Thank you for picking up this book and being willing to consider the beautiful, ugly lessons I offer. I share with you my journey from shadow to light, from hopeless to connected. From my soul to yours, I hope you value the message of transformation and the value of the four pillars I embrace, love, and practice.

PART I

Disconnect

CHAPTER 1

The Forest Through the Trees

"THE MOMENT OF SURRENDER IS NOT WHEN LIFE IS OVER. IT'S WHEN IT BEGINS."
~ MARIANNE WILLIAMSON

"GOD, IF YOU ARE REAL, I NEED HELP."

I was a bit surprised as I heard myself say these words aloud as I looked across the hundreds of treetops on that cold and gray morning in Sacramento. The balcony of our little second-floor apartment was as close to privacy as I was going to get at that moment, and I needed it. I could not look even myself in the eye, much less anyone else. The depth of my aloneness in that moment was like an icy wind blowing through a hole in my soul, and it burned.

My physical body was cold, though. I wrapped my jacket a bit tighter, trying to get warm, perhaps trying to feel held in my moment of extreme shame and bewilderment at my own behavior from the night before. If I could name the feeling in one word, it would be *lost*.

I lived with one of my closest friends from high school, Bonnie, and her mother in a small two-bedroom apartment in Sacramento. They were both home that Saturday morning, and there was no escaping the fact that they remembered the night before better than I did. I had glimpses, but nothing more—a few vague memories of my yelling and throwing something, yet I couldn't tell you what I was mad about. I knew they were both upset with me, and as I stood on the balcony wishing I could disappear, I felt more shame and humiliation than on any other morning after a blackout drunk than I had ever felt before.

There I was for at least the fifth time since I'd moved in, trying to piece together my insane behavior from the night before, recognizing I had been out of control, loud, and volatile, hurting people I cared about once again. These people took me in to support me as I started a new chapter in my life. They trusted me to share their home, and I caused significant disruption to the peaceful home they provided. I created tension, fear, and anger, and I didn't even remember what had happened the night before.

I hated myself. I hated what I mutated into when I drank. I hated not drinking and trying to face even the most mundane activities of everyday life without some form of chemical alteration.

I knew I needed to apologize for my behavior. I knew I needed to stop drinking. I knew I could not yet go back into the apartment, even though I was beginning to really feel the cold and couldn't stay out there much longer.

I pondered the words I'd just spoken to a source I knew nothing about. I hadn't known or experienced anything substantial about religion or spirituality. I didn't have any specific experience with prayer, but I felt compelled to at least try connecting with God, whatever that may be.

My mind took me to the memory of asking my grandmother what religion we were when I was about twelve. I remembered her answer vividly. "Well, I am a Methodist. Your grandfather was Jewish. But all you need to know is that God loves you and He will always forgive you."

I took a deep breath and looked up. The trees in Sacramento were a sight. The palm trees were the most pronounced, but there were several other species as well. There was a sea of green around and above the buildings that surrounded the area. The sky was gray and solemn. My soul, also gray and solemn. Yet, I felt the beauty. I don't know if it was the beauty of the trees or the beauty of an awareness that maybe there was something or someone that might actually hear me. For a split second, I had hope.

My shame drowned it out, but for that split second, there was hope.

I mustered up the courage to go inside, and Bonnie and her mom were in the kitchen. I stood at the edge of the kitchen and offered as sincere an apology as I could. I'd considered sharing with them that I had prayed, but the look on their faces was both disgust and worry, so I spoke as briefly as possible and just hung my head and went to lie down.

Bonnie wasn't overly religious, but she had a deep love for Jesus and the Bible—I'm sure her mother did, too. So, the idea of sharing that I had prayed felt like an attempt to manipulate the situation and somehow redeem it. But I didn't want redemption at that moment. I wanted to hate myself and my life, and I wanted them to hate me, too.

There's much about that time that's a bit foggy. I had just turned twenty and had only been in Sacramento for a few months. I'd moved there under the premise that I was going to start my life on a good foot. I had just completed my vocational training in Job Corps, and Bonnie invited me to come to California to live with her and her mom, get a good job, make better decisions than I'd made in Colorado, and keep my act together.

However, my migration toward alcohol and drugs, and those who enjoyed abusing them with me, ran deep.

My plan wasn't going too well.

During my first few weeks in California, I did get a job, but it was with a bunch of partiers who drove cars for under-the-table cash for local car dealers and body shops. I didn't even have a legal driver's license, but the job paid cash. It completely sidetracked me from my efforts to find an office job, but it kept me close to my conditioned and self-abusive ways of substance abuse.

Waking up in a fog about the night before was all too familiar. I had been doing it since I was twelve years old. However, waking up in a fog and breaking so many promises to myself after the big idea of my new life in California, which had been a dream for all of my teen years, hit a whole new level of humiliation and self-degradation.

In many moments of self-punishment, I pushed myself to get out and look for a real job. I'd wake up with world-class hangovers and angry roommates; I'd apologize, shower, get dolled up, and leave to look for places to apply or submit a résumé.

I wish I could tell you that particular morning was the last time I had apologized to them for my horrible behavior. I wish I could say that was the day I got sober, and all of my drunken mayhem, recklessness, selfishness, and self-sabotage ended right there, but that's not the case.

That morning was different because it included not only an awareness that I needed help but also a plea to God. I can't say that I even knew if the apologies I made to them, myself, or anyone had any merit at the time. I can only say that my despair was increasing. I knew I was a failure.

I had failed at starting my new life. I had failed at managing my drinking. I had failed my dear friend and her mother, whom

I respected and loved, and who had so graciously taken me in. And if there *was* a God, I was undoubtedly failing Him. I knew something had to give, but I was just lost. I had so many intentions for a fresh start in California, yet there I was, equally as out of control as I was in Colorado.

My prayer that morning was the beginning of my spiritual awakening. I didn't know it that day or even for many weeks to come, but I can say with great conviction today that *that* prayer brought many synchronicities shortly after, which led me to the life I have today. I have no doubt that God, Source, The Creator, or whatever Divine Intelligence you may call by name, is up there, has a much more powerful plan than anything I could dream up, and my gratitude for that plan goes beyond any words I could share with you.

Chapter 2
Little Hands, Big Burdens

"Now every time I witness a strong person, I want to know: What darkness did you conquer in your story? Mountains do not rise without earthquakes."
~ Katherine MacKenett

The majority of the alcoholics and addicts I know have something in common: a sensitive soul that was traumatized in some way, physically, mentally, emotionally, sexually, or otherwise, that caused a deep, internal disconnect from Source and others. This disconnect can create a sense of isolation and aloneness that is so painful, it may feel like an icy wind blowing through an open wound. The natural instinct is to escape the pain. This was certainly my experience in the early years of my life.

So, I'll start from the beginning.

My mother was only nineteen and on her second marriage when she got pregnant with me. At just nineteen years old, she had already been married, divorced, and had had a child almost three years earlier. And her second marriage was failing.

She had been working as a truck stop waitress when she fell in love with a truck mechanic who was married with two children and one on the way, a man who had no intention of leaving his family.

When she told him she was pregnant with me, he and his family moved, never to be heard from again. Her current husband, the man named on my birth certificate, filed for divorce when I was two months old, as he found out about the affair and knew I was not his child. He was heard from again, but only to maintain that he knew he was not the father. My mother had also confirmed this several times, so I certainly understand his stance and the cause of the divorce.

So, at just nineteen years old, she had a toddler and a new baby, and she was alone. When I stand in her shoes, I feel the disconnect. I feel the aloneness, fear, self-criticism (at best), and hurt. At just a few weeks in gestation, I also acknowledge that my tiny being felt all of that with her.

My mother's third marriage, when I was not yet three, was to a psychopathic alcoholic who was extremely unstable, angry, and had a pretty severe history of his own abuse.

The next few years were horrifying.

It's not uncommon to have little memory of early childhood, but the memories of my small body being violated and tossed around, physically and metaphorically, are a little hazy. I recall many of the feelings, but not many of the details of the actual events. As someone who has done a great deal of healing work over many years, I realize it is not an uncommon thing to subconsciously "brown out" memories from a traumatic childhood.

What I do remember is that I was four years old when my younger brother, Jeffrey, was born, and the memories of our home from that time are a mixed bag of being a small child who didn't know any better and a terrified soul who knew something was terribly wrong in our home.

I have always been very empathic and could feel my mother's tension from another room. I would feel compelled to check on her. Even as a very small child, I felt a deep need to take care of her. If I interrupted an argument, scolding, or beating from my stepfather, I became the target of his anger or rage and took my own beatings.

There were times she tried to defend me and times that she was relieved someone came to her aid, even if that someone was her small child. I didn't have any real way to gauge the degree of danger I was putting myself in. I'm not sure I cared. I wanted to protect her.

My older sister, Lorri, tried to protect me by holding me back. She'd make me hide with her when the raging would begin. We hid behind clothes in the back of closets, under dirty laundry, in tandem with stuffed animals, and even once, my sister told me to hide behind the pipes under the kitchen sink in the cabinet. We knew not to hide under the bed, as it was too easy for him to find us.

We were clever and imaginative for our own survival, and he became even more so in his pursuit. I can't count the number of bruises, welts, or terrifying moments from his beatings or him throwing Lorri or me across a room.

It was a time of chaos, fear, and abuse in every form imaginable. As a child, I was deeply conflicted about what love was. I was told to call a man who hurt my mother, my sister, and me in terrible ways, "Dad." The only thing I was not conflicted about was knowing he was *not* my father.

I witnessed his love for my younger brother, and while the majority of my memories are sadness, abuse, and terror, I do remember seeing beyond the surface of this very scary man's soul. He was tortured. He hated himself and took it out on everyone. He would put on a fake smile in public and then be a monster at home.

One morning, another "morning after," I saw him sitting on the sofa in the living room with his head in his hands. He was crying. My empathic nature felt his shame and self-loathing. I don't remember being told anything about his childhood, but in my mind's eye, I saw a little boy being beaten and manipulated in the same ways he had done to my mother, sister, and me.

I had an overwhelming moment of compassion for him. It was a deeply conflicting energy of fear to approach and an inability not to. I knew how quickly my decision could go wrong, but the immature child in me who sought love so desperately also gave love without much thought.

So, I slowly walked up to him and stood about two feet away. I was just looking at him and wondering if I should try to comfort him when he looked up and saw me. I was so frightened when he looked at me, but I could not help but put my hands on his face. I was frozen and unable to say what my heart was feeling. I just wanted to tell him he didn't have to be so angry, but I knew not to say a word.

Within moments, I felt his energy of embarrassment that a little girl was seeing his shame, and I tried to step back as I was so frightened by the sudden shift. The look on his face went from "Thank you for seeing me" to "How dare you look into me?"

He loved the power he had over our fear. He popped his face very close to mine and said, "Boo!" knowing I was frightened, and I ran to my room. I never approached him in those moments like that again. I felt them but never risked that intense polar duality again.

I was eight years old when we escaped.

We lived in Texas, a place that I still struggle to visit. Aunt Carmen had visited my mom from Colorado, and they went to

Mexico for a few days. They returned with trinkets, gifts for all of us, and a large, beautiful vase that was taller than me. My mother was so excited about the deals she'd gotten and talked about how worried she had been about getting the vase home without breaking it.

It was probably three to four feet tall and was a white ceramic vase with beautiful blue floral designs that were right about my chin. I loved it, too, and wondered what she could put in there that would be tall enough. I was happy for her and her treasure.

It wasn't but moments after my aunt left to return to Colorado that he started in on her, asking how much she had spent and who they had met while they were there. He was always suspicious and controlling of her every move. It was one of the worst fights I'd ever seen them have. He threw her small body across the hall into the pretty vase, causing it to shatter across the entire hallway where she had placed it. I felt her heart break as profoundly as the vase. There was no question that shattering the vase was his intention.

My sister, brother, and I had been hiding in a bedroom at the end of the hall where she had placed the vase. He had picked her up, and they had gone into the kitchen, where he continued to berate and beat her. So, I ran down the hall through the many small pieces of the vase to the front door to get help. We lived on the second floor, and the stairs were about three feet in front of our door. It took me a moment to get the door open, which gave him time to realize what I was doing, so he came after me. I made it out the door and had just rounded the first steps down when I felt myself being pulled back by my hair, and I felt the corner of the metal railing running up my back, so I screamed. He slammed the front door and threw me down the hall amid the fragments of the vase and turned his rage on me.

My mother was screaming at him to stop when someone pounded on the front door.

The commotion had caught a neighbor's attention, and they had come to help. He opened the door shirtless and yelled at them to mind their own business, then slammed the door again.

He settled down, because I'm sure he was embarrassed that a neighbor had heard him. I was thankful that he snapped out of it, but the mess in the house was awful: vase fragments, food, and broken dishes thrown across the kitchen floor and counters, and the soda dripping down the wall from where he'd thrown it. My mom was shaking and trying so hard not to break down as she cleaned up the pieces of her new vase. She had a few minor cuts just below her eye, and her makeup was smeared, and through a steady stream of tears, she kept whispering, "I'm sorry. I'm so sorry," to my sister, brother, and me.

Very early that following morning, while it was still dark, she woke us all up, whispering for us to go to the car. None of us asked why or flinched; we just knew to run to the car. In the middle of December 1975, we escaped that apartment, that terror, and that marriage in our pajamas.

We pulled into Aunt Carmen and Uncle Chuck's home just after nightfall. It was a very cold and snowy night in Colorado, and my uncle carried us from the car to the front door because we didn't have shoes.

My aunt and uncle helped my mom get on her feet, and we moved into an apartment. She became a single mom, and we became latchkey kids. And the fear and terror of living with a very abusive man was over. A new set of challenges was before us, but none compared to the terror he put all of us through.

There are several more stories of physical, sexual, mental, and emotional abuse from those years of my life that I'm sure would make anyone's blood boil. They would make a person want to prosecute this man and a few others. They would stir anger at my mother for not leaving sooner or for not protecting her children or herself. But stories like mine are unfortunately not as uncommon as we would all like them to be, and I've painted the picture clearly enough. And honestly, I don't wish to leave more of an imprint than I already have.

This part of my childhood was brutal. The highly sensitive little girl who could not protect herself or her family grew up feeling a sense of failure, self-hatred, unworthiness, and, yes, alone and disconnected. She didn't know what a peaceful night of sleep was like, as she had to be on guard relentlessly. The conditioning of anxiety and fear ran deep. There was a very distorted sense of reality as to what a "normal" family should be.

CHAPTER 3

An Above-Average Dysfunctional Family

"THE THING ABOUT CHAOS IS THAT WHILE IT DISTURBS US, IT TOO
FORCES OUR HEARTS TO ROAR IN A WAY WE SECRETLY FIND
MAGNIFICENT."
~ CHRISTOPHER POINDEXTER

"DAMN IT!" SHE YELLED as she threw the car back in park and flung the driver's door open. Her small, skinny frame stormed into the house and returned a few seconds later with oven mitts on and the casserole that had been cooking. She yelled at us to hit the button that would pop the trunk open, and a few seconds later, we heard it slam shut. She got back in the car, quickly pulled out, and we were barreling down the road.

Just like early childhood, the years and holidays are a bit of a haze, but I'm sure it was Thanksgiving or Christmas. We were headed to one of the big family gatherings that were a norm throughout our childhood.

Mom always stressed over family get-togethers. She would fret over how the gifts were wrapped, complain about how much things cost, or mutter, "Michael better not be there."

Often, in the weeks leading up to any gathering, there were several overheard conversations about telling either my uncle

Michael or my aunt Devona that we weren't doing anything or any number of lies to keep them from coming. Those two often took the heat for the out-of-control behavior that extreme substance abuse can cause, but I want to state clearly here that it wasn't *just* them.

I don't know much about how they all got along as my mother was growing up, but I know there were rifts between many of them in adulthood, and the one thing most of them had in common, severe abuse of alcohol and drugs, didn't help matters.

The nervousness she would exhibit on the way to these occasions was always noticeable. I believe they truly loved one another, but the tension was just as true. It caused her to want everything to be just so.

She taught me how to iron my clothes almost as soon as I was tall enough to reach the ironing board, as it was important to her that we all looked clean, well-groomed, and better than any of her siblings' kids. She would remind us to chew with our mouths closed and to say please and thank you. She warned us that if we fought during the party, there'd be hell to pay when we got home.

I grin a little when I think about her threats. She never laid a hand on us, and although she could act a bit erratic and yell a lot, she never once scared me. My younger inner child knows fear, but this chapter is dedicated to my slightly older inner child, who knew freedom from severe abuse. I didn't know peace, security, or have much of a semblance of what living in a home with emotional connection was like, but freedom from severe abuse was a gift that I treasured.

I was about eleven years old. I remember sitting in the back seat with what seemed like natural amnesia about the last family gathering and looking forward to getting there. It didn't matter whose house we were headed to; I just knew my mother's extended family would be there, there would be a ton of good food, and my grandmother would be elated to see me.

The family I grew up with was entirely on my maternal side. My mother had six brothers and sisters. They bore my grandmother sixteen grandchildren. All seven of the siblings on my mother's side worked in the restaurant and bar industry. They could cook, had great humor (and sarcasm), and were all very good-looking people by society's standards.

When we arrived that day, most of the family was already there. Aunt Carmen and Uncle Chuck held these gatherings most often, as they had the biggest house. There were probably twenty-five to thirty of us, and it was loud. We walked in, and the smell of homemade everything was wondrous! My first stop was to find my grandmother and give her a hug. She was the main cook of the house, so it was brief, but she always stopped whatever she was doing to hug me.

Then came the rounds with the other aunts, uncles, and cousins, along with all the comments about how much older I looked and how long my hair had grown. The love at the beginning of these events was my favorite part. I knew it could all go south by the time we got to the dessert, but I loved arriving and how jovial it was.

Food was spread throughout the kitchen and onto the separate dining room area table, which seated twenty. Two kids' tables were also in the kitchen area. Every table was set to perfection, with linens, nice table settings, and floral arrangements on the main table.

Initially, there was a ton of laughter and joking, and everyone looked so nice in their holiday best. As we finally sat down for dinner, the food was laid out across the long table; I sat in an end chair because I am left-handed and didn't want to bump into anyone while eating.

We started to pass the food, and my aunt Devona commented, "Shouldn't we say grace?"

After some reluctance and indecision about who should lead prayer, Uncle Michael cut in with, "Jesus, just get it over with."

Everyone quickly took hands while Devona said a short and sweet prayer with hurt feelings.

That was the first tiff of the day.

I liked praying in unison, even though I didn't really understand it. The sound of the voices saying "Amen" together just felt good to me, so I was happy we did, but we could all feel the conflicted tension at the table.

As we passed the food, there was a mix of good manners and raised voices asking for the gravy, butter, or salt. Rather than passing the basket, a dinner roll or two was thrown to someone. It was lively and loud, and while there would be a sneer or two and many sarcastic jabs at one another, everyone was excited to eat together and share in all of the craft that went into preparing it. There was always an incredible spread, and literally each bite, flavor, and texture was delectable. My family had many good cooks.

After dinner, at least six people packed leftovers and washed dishes, and ten others complained a little more about how much they'd eaten. Once the cleanup was finished, those over thirteen took their place around the long dining room table and grabbed their bingo card. At this point, not only were the desserts up for grabs, but the booze had its own special lineup.

The kids had the option to go off and play together, or we could hang out in the dining room and watch the bingo game as we ate as many servings of dessert as we could.

I loved seeing my cousins. We played games, ate together, joked, and picked on each other just like the adults did, but after dinner, I almost always ended up sitting by my grandmother.

She didn't play. She just chain-smoked, drank black coffee, and sometimes vodka, and enjoyed being with her family. I enjoyed being near her. So, I ate dessert, watched the game and the drinking, and noticed the voices and tensions rise. A part of me sat by her to assure her that even if it went bad, I was there for her.

"Bingo!" yelled two voices at the same time. Rather than a little friendly gameplay competition, it became sibling rivalry to a highly volatile degree. My uncle Renee was the sorest loser and often had the sharpest sarcasm. "Let the bitch have it so she doesn't cry," he said as he stood up and threw his bingo card across the table.

My aunt Devona gave him the death stare.

My mother looked at her and sneered, "Don't be such a baby."

"Knock it off!" Uncle Michael shoved Renee's shoulder, attempting to push him out of the dining room. But it had begun. They all started arguing with one another. They had been drinking most of the afternoon, and many were drunk. Their judgment was impaired, and the unresolved hurts of many years past, which had nothing to do with who won at bingo, erupted.

"Take it outside!" yelled Uncle Chuck, over slurred profanities, tears, pushing, and hitting. He didn't want something to get broken.

I just held my grandmother's hand and said, "Let's go to the living room." She stood up, and we walked into the other room while those who were a bit less interested in joining the shouting match started to clear the table.

"Your uncle is such an asshole," my mother said while putting on her coat. "Go get your brother and sister."

And just like that, the holiday was over.

As another family gathering that had started off well fell apart, the two things I remember the most are the horrified disappointment on my grandmother's face and the knowledge that the ride home was going to be laden with Mom's dramatic tears and yelling about the whole family.

This was such a common experience that we all normalized it. Lorri, Jeffrey, and I would ride home in silence, just letting her rant.

Shortly after arriving home, Mom would make a phone call or two and then tell us she was going out.

We were left to our own devices, and we weren't well-equipped to be without supervision.

Mom left, and my sister took the phone to her room, shutting the door behind her. At fourteen, she spent a lot of time on the phone. I went to my room, followed by my brother. He wanted to play a game. I tried to tell him to go watch TV, but he grabbed my hand and said "Please?" with his big brown eyes, so we got out some cards and went to the living room.

After several rounds of Go Fish, I was growing bored and Lorri had come to the kitchen for a snack, so I tried to get her to take over.

"I'm busy," she said.

"Aw, c'mon! It's your turn." I said, knowing she would understand it was her turn to hang with Jeffrey.

"He's a big boy. I'm going to my room."

"Bitch," I said somewhat under my breath but loud enough for her to hear me.

"What did you say?!" She started walking toward the living room.

"Nothing. Just go to your room." My heart began to race a little. I hadn't expected to anger her so quickly, but there was no backing down now.

I tried to stand up before she got to me, but she pushed me to the floor and punched me in the head. I kicked her in the belly, and she almost fell back but caught herself and came lunging at me again. My brother moved over to the recliner chair, and I caught a glimpse of his face as we were attacking each other and shouting all the profanities we could think of.

"Stop! Stop! Stop!" Jeffrey shouted at the top of his young lungs and started to cry.

"See what you did?!" I yelled at her.

"Fuck you! You started it!"

"Fuck *you!*"

She grabbed the phone receiver and threw it at my head. "Ow!" I grabbed my head and went to my knees.

"Stop! Stop! Stop!" Jeffrey yelled again through his tears.

Lorri finally realized she'd snapped and needed to stop.

"I'm sorry. I'm so sorry," she said as she came to me and tried to check my head and make sure she hadn't hurt me too badly.

"Just leave me alone," I said in a quieter tone. "I'm fine."

She went to our brother, hugged him, and told him she was sorry, and I began to straighten up the cards and coffee table that had gotten moved out of place.

The violence was over, and it was quiet for a minute. Lorri got me ice for the growing knot on my head, and we directed our attention to Jeffrey.

"You still want to play Fish?"

He was hesitant and still a bit shaken. He took a minute to think about it before he answered. "Okay," he said, and my sister began to shuffle the cards.

We played cards, ate potato chips, drank sodas, and checked the knot on my head a few times. It wasn't any serious injury, just a moment of volatility that turned into three siblings playing Go Fish and watching *Laverne & Shirley*.

It's not too unlike the adults who raised us, who would all love each other at the beginning of the next holiday dinner.

My siblings and I shared some special moments and selfish, immature outbursts as children with very little supervision. We were alone a lot. We made our way with fights, many moments of isolation in our own rooms, or absorbed in a TV show. We knew how to make basic meals like sandwiches, scrambled eggs, or cereal, and we ate alone a lot.

All the surface essentials were in place. Mom provided food, clothing, and shelter, but emotional stability and guidance were running on fumes. She faced many struggles of her own with her siblings, money management, relationships, and, mostly, her health. I truly can't recall any period where Mom didn't have some looming health issue.

She was born with one kidney, so she indeed had some very real health issues. She had a weak immune system, and her life-style of working in a bar and often drinking too much didn't help. Living much of her life as unwell, she always feared, and even expected, to be ill, and often she was.

I was about seven when I learned what the word *hypochondriac* meant. I understood that many of my mother's ailments were imagined, but I also worried about her deeply. Real or imagined, she truly *believed* she was ill. She was scared, uncomfortable, and often visibly unwell. She had a lot of doctor's appointments and often missed work.

When she wasn't too sick to get out of bed, she would leave around four o'clock and get home around two a.m. (on the nights she came home). She often came in drunk and stumbling and, now and again, really angry about the state of the house. Many nights, we woke up after midnight to yelling, something breaking, or the need to escape a messy situation Mom had created with the landlord.

Emotional instability wasn't the only issue. Residential, educational, and financial instability were all up there, too.

We would pack up and move to a new home every six to nine months. We moved several times. Once, it was because she couldn't pay the rent. Another time, we had a ghost. A few times, we moved to a nicer place because Mom's boyfriend had given her the money to afford it. How long we'd stay in any given home was always up in the air, but to her credit, we did have shelter. And from her perspective, that was what mattered most.

Of course, with the frequent moves came frequent changes in schools. When I started my second middle school at twelve, I remember being called into the counselor's office for a new-student meeting. I had been to many schools before but had not had this kind of meeting. At first, I was a little flattered that a counselor wanted to meet me just because I was new. I thought that was a cool thing the new school did for all the new kids.

After a few general questions and after observing that I had switched schools often, the counselor asked, "So, can you tell me about your home life?

I was taken aback as I wasn't going to answer that honestly. "It's fine."

"Is your mom the only adult who lives there?"

"Yes."

"Do you get along?"

"Yes. She works a lot, but we're close," I lied. I fully understood the reason for this meeting was not to welcome me to the school, but to investigate my background since I'd transferred schools so much. A part of me was surprised that someone noticed. Another part of me was terrified that if she knew the truth about my mother's drinking or the history with my stepfather or how we were alone most of the time, there would be a risk of being taken away.

"I'm glad to hear that. When I saw how many schools you attended, I wanted to meet you to ensure that everything at home was okay. I wanted to make sure you knew that if you ever needed to talk to someone, you knew where to go."

"Thank you. That's nice. Everything is good, though." I smiled as sincerely as I could, hoping this was the end of it. But no...

"So, where is your father?"

"He lives in Oklahoma."

"That must be hard."

"Yeah. He is my stepdad, and we go visit him there." I fumbled a little with this quick-witted lie, but venturing anywhere near the truth was not an option. Any questions about my father were extremely uncomfortable. I feared that if she knew the reality of the years with my stepfather or that I hadn't ever even met my birth father, it would have led to a child services investigation. Even though our home wasn't perfect, this conversation gave me a whole new fear about being taken away from it.

I made friends with kids who had lived in the same school system and even in the same house their entire lives. I realized they had had a very different experience from mine, one of stability and security. The beauty of that awareness was recognizing that there was a better normal than what I had known. But I struggled deeply to feel like I fit in or belonged anywhere because of this, and I was cautious with every word I spoke to kids my own age, just as I was with adults. The fear of their judgment or of their knowing truths about my life was always present.

I consistently felt that I would probably leave these circles soon, so I didn't really connect with anyone too deeply.

Disconnect was the conditioning we witnessed in the adults who never talked it out with any maturity. The example of escapism into severe alcohol and drug use by these same adults was more proof of disconnect. Moving from place to place on impulse was another one. All these examples of disconnect turned into isolation in our own young lives, which was so familiar that it was comfortable. Not healthy, but it was what we adapted to.

When I reflect on my family and upbringing, I can't help but laugh a little when I use the phrase *above-average dysfunctional family*. While it would feel like a typical day when the rug was ripped out from under us, causing a sudden change or chaos, I also grew to realize it wasn't that way for everyone. I knew that our life had been a roller coaster of instability that could be classed as neglect, discipline that could be charged as abuse, and numerous extremely inappropriate experiences of language and physical touch that could call for a child to be removed from a home by current-day standards. It was beyond dysfunction, but I soften it by saying it was an *above-average dysfunctional family*. That covers a great deal of ground, with far less discomfort.

CHAPTER 4
Diary of a Rag Doll

"WHATEVER'S WORRYING YOU RIGHT NOW, FORGET ABOUT IT.
THINK OF SOMEONE WHO MAKES YOU FEEL SAFE AND LOVED.
BREATHE IN THIS LOVE."
~ KAREN SALMANSOHN

AS A SMALL CHILD, I EXPERIENCED moments of fear, hatred, and hopelessness, where I cursed my life and my parental figures, realizing that whatever was the opposite was what I longed for in my future. I also noted what life was like in the homes of those friends I had made in the various schools and neighborhoods we lived in. They were brief views, but there were homes with two parents (even some who liked each other) and friends who still occupied the same bedrooms they had had when they were born. These friends had other friends they had known their entire lives and parents they trusted. My admiration for that depth of history left an indelible mark on my heart and soul.

I knew I would grow up and have the choice to break the chains of disconnection, struggle, and severe alcohol and drug use that I'd seen in the generation above mine. I knew my rag doll life, of being tossed about thoughtlessly, would one day change.

While some childhood memories are blocked and hazy, I clearly remember daydreaming as I stared out a window or played on the playground. I couldn't help but think about my reality, especially the wild emotions and overreactions I witnessed in my family's adults, but those memories stood in contrast to my imagination.

I'd experienced and witnessed a lot of discord and abuse with adults, so I'd imagine many ideals of healthier parents or couples who laughed together, cooked together, or built a swing set together in the backyard, holding the pieces in place, and handing each other tools in a manner that was cooperative and amicable.

I had known many different home styles and good and bad neighborhoods, most of which I didn't get enough time to truly explore. Sometimes, we never even fully unpacked. So, I envisioned a stable, long-term home with many pictures on the wall, where everything had a place—not in a cardboard box. I had a vision of fresh flowers in vases and a soft blanket on the corner of a sofa.

I'd known a great deal of shouting, slamming, breakage, and other noises, like the sounds of a grown man's footsteps approaching my bed as I slept, so a favorite vision was of being a mother and seeing my own child sleeping safely with a cute nightlight softly lighting their room in case they woke. In some moments, I would close my eyes and could truly *feel* this picture of a house that was a sacred space with love, comfort, and security. I may have seen something similar in a TV show or movie, but when I saw it in my mind's eye, I could feel it.

In reflection, I often wonder if my intuition, the witnessing of stability in my friends' homes, or my connection to my grandmother influenced my ability to daydream about a better future. I cannot begin to articulate my gratitude for all of these daydreams, no matter where they were rooted, as I know that they saved my soul and fueled the Divine's intervention.

The divine intervention in my childhood was my grandmother. She was this lighthouse that guided me to shore on numerous occasions when I was lost. She was a secret hideout. She was many other metaphors for the hero of the story and a safe place. I could truly write an entire book just in tribute to her and how my experiences of this singular connection became paramount.

When I was younger, she was in our lives off and on, typically during the times when she and my mother got along. If they were speaking and she was around, I could breathe better.

She had sixteen grandchildren and made no bones about sharing that I was her favorite. I'll admit that I wish she hadn't been so bold about that in front of my siblings or cousins, as some resented me, for she wasn't as kind to them. But being her favorite was also this special place that often felt like the only safe place in the world.

We truly enjoyed one another's company, doing just about anything. When I was small and before we had moved to Texas, I would stay with her in her small one-bedroom apartment. Sometimes, it was a single night. Other times, it was a week. She didn't drive, so we just found things to do while at her home.

I was never a good sleeper, so while she slept, I would be awake, opening drawers and cabinets and exploring every little item she had. She had a lot of mementos, and nothing was out of place. Pictures of family members were in frames. Her clothes were hung in her closet, and hat boxes were on the shelves at the top. The only thing on her closet floor was shoes. I would unfold a piece of clothing, attempt to fold it the same way, and put it back once I'd seen what it looked like. I'd touch every piece of her jewelry and hold it up to myself as I looked in the mirror.

She had a beautiful vanity with makeup and perfumes, and I'd open every lipstick and powder case to smell them. I never put any of it on, but I wanted to know the smells, colors, and textures. There was no limit, other than what I couldn't reach, that I didn't want to touch and get to know.

One morning when I had spent the night, she was getting a few things out of the refrigerator to make breakfast and she said, "I know you were looking through my things."

I immediately blushed and became nervous, as I thought I was about to get in trouble with her for the first time. I never had any ill intent; I was just deeply curious. "Yes," I said, ready to take whatever punishment she would give. I wasn't afraid of her, so admission was very natural.

"Why?" She looked over at me, genuinely interested in my answer.

"I don't know," was the best I could offer. At that time, I honestly didn't know why I wanted to touch, feel, smell, and experience everything there was to explore about her.

She must have sensed that I was really unsure about my intention because she then asked me if I wanted poached eggs for breakfast, which are my favorite. Then she dropped the question and brought me a cup of orange juice.

However, that question rang in my thoughts for years. I felt guilty for going through her things as I had. I wondered if she might have perceived it as some kind of violation of her privacy. Yet, I remember every smell, texture, and smile I had when I explored.

I was in my twenties when I realized the answer; it was because I wanted to know what it was about me that made me her favorite. I tried to figure her out. I didn't feel special to any other adult. I was abandoned, abused, and told that I was bad in a thousand ways, and yet, I could do no wrong in my grandmother's eyes. I was conditioned to believe that I was a burden, I was too expensive, and that I was too sensitive, but she had never once told me anything of this nature. She fawned over me like I was a precious treasure, especially if I was ill.

In fact, there were several times that I wondered how many of her own children, especially my mother, could be so messed up with her as their mother. I wondered if she had rubbed my mother's feet the way she had rubbed mine, or if she had gently laid a blanket over her own children and kissed them on the forehead the way she had me so many times as I was going to bed, had a cold, or even if I was just sitting by the television. Reconciling the way that she was a grandmother to me and wondering how she was a mother to her own children was never something I could do.

As she aged and became less capable, she moved in with Aunt Carmen and Uncle Chuck and their three sons. When my grandmother was at our home or I was with her at my aunt and uncle's, I always slept with her.

She would put on her face cream and nightgown, open the window just a crack, saying, "This is the trick to the best sleep," and turn off the light. As our eyes adjusted to the dark of night, I could smell her face cream as we lay facing each other, holding hands, and we would talk. Sometimes just for a few moments, other times, late into the night. These are the most cherished moments of my childhood and later became guiding posts to the rest of my life.

I often wonder if my brother or sister had anyone to have secret conversations with, who gave them permission to say anything they wanted, even curse words, about all the anger or instability they felt about our mother or our home life.

In contrast to the beautiful angel-like being that I knew my grandmother to be, she was fairly harsh to my mother. I have to admit that I was conflicted when they argued. My grandmother was very critical of my mother's choices, and while she wasn't wrong, her presentation was gruff, to say the least.

My mother felt that providing shelter, food, and clothing was her primary role. Being present emotionally, providing stability beyond the minimal food and shelter requirements, or caring about how her choices affected her children, sincerely did not occur to her. She was a well-known bartender in Denver, and she had a great love for her customers and employers. It fed a part of her that needed attention and connection and that the responsibility of motherhood didn't offer, especially after her third divorce, when she was a single mother again.

My reflection of my mother from our childhood is filled with so much awareness of how not to raise a child, but the moments of light that were my imagination, my spirit, and my grandmother are in that reflection, too. There are moments of being hurt and angry, and then moments of dancing and laughing in the living room while my grandmother told me what an amazing dancer I was.

As I reflect on the adoration I had for my grandmother and the connection we shared, I remember how loved I felt. I remember feeling like I had this sacred place that only she and I knew about.

When I think about a diary, I think of writing down any thoughts that come to mind in a private place where no one will read them. It is a place to write about dreams, hopes, bad days, and the moments that bring joy. A diary allows the writer to vent, write about when life hurts, and process bewilderment.

My grandmother *was* my diary. She carried my truths in words I never had to speak. She was entrusted with my deepest soul, and even though she isn't still with us, she still is.

CHAPTER 5

Make it Stop

"SHE WORE A THOUSAND FACES ALL TO HIDE HER OWN."
~ ATTICUS

ONE NIGHT, WHEN OUR MOTHER was at work, my sister snuck in some boys with beer, and I heard them all come in, so I went to see who it was. When I opened my door, I saw the beers and told my sister I wanted one. She said I could have one if I promised I wouldn't tell Mom that she had friends over, to which I readily agreed.

I was twelve, Lorri was fifteen. She had cool friends, long, pretty hair, and many tricks up her sleeve to fool any adult. I admired all of these things about her. Just a few months earlier, she had yelled at me about how immature I was, so becoming cool was pretty high on my priority list.

I had always been a very sensitive soul, but puberty had introduced even bigger emotions. I had started stewing in self-pity and anger about the many memories of our earlier life that often would pummel me as if I were still living them. The need to be distracted or simply forget our past was almost constant. And, of course, I wanted my older sister to think I was mature,

I wanted her friends to like me, and I wanted to do anything I could to escape my emotions and life in general.

My sister went into her room with one of the boys, and the other boy and I sat on the floor in the unfinished part of the basement that we had made into a living room. We had a full sofa facing a wall where there was a huge stereo system we had gotten at a yard sale. Next to the stereo case was a stack of vinyl albums from all of our favorite artists, such as Journey, Styx, Billy Joel, REO Speedwagon, and Pat Benatar. We taped a couple of posters on the wall of the same bands and had a lava lamp on the one tall speaker. It was pretty dimly lit as we only hung out in that area to listen to music.

Lorri's friend had been smoking pot along with the beer and was pretty stoned. He was just lying back in the corner of the couch with his eyes closed, just nodding his head to the music while I drank my beer and watched the purple light of the lava lamp reflect on the dimly lit wall. When I finished it, I asked him to hand me another one, and he barely opened his eyes as he handed it over. I felt like I was one of the cool kids. Lorri and her boyfriend came out and we all sat around drinking beer, playing records, and I just listened while they talked. I didn't want to say something awkward because I had no idea what "mature" really meant, but I didn't want to mess it up.

I remember counting the beers as I opened them. They were the tallboy cans, and I drank them as fast as I could. I have no idea what time it was, but I had four and a half before I started to feel nauseous.

I weighed maybe ninety pounds and had never been drunk before. I had snuck a drink or two at our family gatherings but had never gotten drunk. But on this night, it was game on. I had seen members of my family drunk many times, but I never understood what took the adults I'd known from coherent, reasonable, and funny to drunk with a totally different personality. I'd wondered what the big deal was since it seemed to hold a high priority for the adults around me. And now Lorri was drinking. I knew she smoked a lot of pot and that she smoked cigarettes, which I had a curiosity about already, but I hadn't seen her drink.

I was very clear in my mind that I intended to get drunk. I didn't know exactly what it meant beyond what I had witnessed, but I wanted to experience it for myself.

And boy, did I...

We didn't have a bathroom in the basement of that house yet, as our bedrooms were the only part of the basement that was finished. So, I ran upstairs to the bathroom and vomited up everything that was in my stomach. I remember feeling a little better after vomiting and going back to the basement for more.

I don't remember if they knew I was sick, if I drank more, or if we were all as drunk because the rest of the night is lost.

I blacked out the very first time I got drunk.

I don't remember if I had a hangover, but I remember I couldn't wait to do it again. There was an appeal to the oblivion I'd experienced that even I didn't understand. All of the sensitivities, heavy emotions, and memories that I'd been forced to disconnect from were shut down by four and a half cans of beer.

It was a disconnect from the disconnect.

This also opened the conversation with my sister about smoking pot. I had a few things over her head from her teenage shenanigans, so she was being a lot nicer to me. I also leveled up to a partner-in-crime status, and she had some things over me, too.

She let me listen to her albums, taught me how to smoke pot and cigarettes, let me drink if her friends were drinking, and we just agreed we wouldn't tell Mom.

And so it began... I found a solution to numb my wounded soul and overly sensitive emotions. I found a way out of the constant triggers and reliving of harsh memories in my head. I found an escape that I'd been seeking for years, and in doing so, I found a deeper bond with my sister that I'd been craving.

I would drink any chance I got. I smoked pot almost every day as my sister sold it and made sure I was always stocked, which was her way of keeping me close and quiet. I did a few favors for her, too, such as chores or taking care of Jeffrey. We had a pretty good deal going on there, and the era of throwing phone receivers and cussing at each other was replaced with stolen glances of knowing we had each other's backs.

Lorri and I both fought with our mother. However, Lorri and our mother fought much worse. Our mother had unrealistic expectations of her. "You're the oldest. You should know better" was relevant to how to clean the house or what she should or shouldn't let me or Jeff do. She was a young teenager who should have been trying to figure out geometry problems, not how to raise a little sister and brother.

My empathy for my sister ran the deepest. I'm sure that's why I also looked up to her. She survived the worst of our stepfather. My witness and memories of the mental, physical, and psychological abuse she took in our early childhood were deeply imprinted in my own soul, so I know how deep the scars were for her. She didn't know any better than I or our little brother. She was just a kid trying to get through another day of mayhem with zero skills or tools on how to manage a house, kids, or the stability our mother expected of her. The role reversal abuse, if we can give that a name, was significant from an early age for all of us.

It was just a few months after that first drink when my mother kicked Lorri out. I came home from school one day, and she was really laying into her.

"You will never live under my roof again! You are nothing but a whore!" She was screaming and throwing things in her room at her. It was the first time I'd seen her attempt any degree of physical harm to one of us.

The look on Lorri's face was both complete terror and relief.

She had gotten pregnant at fifteen. And Mom had no idea how to handle it other than to scream and yell extremely hurtful and punishing words. Lorri never stood a chance to defend herself or be treated with any degree of compassion, discussion, or guidance. The fact that it had never been impressed upon her *not* to get pregnant was disregarded entirely.

Mom continued to rant more harshly, shouting continuous below-the-belt statements and calling Lorri names that no mother should ever consider, much less scream in rage. She made it very clear that having an abortion was the only choice in the matter and then laid the final blow that Lorri was no longer her daughter and needed to get the hell out.

Uncle Chuck pulled up, and Lorri had been looking out the window, waiting for him. I didn't get to hug her or say goodbye. She just walked as quickly as she could to his truck the second he was in view.

It was a sudden and significant change that I wasn't ready for. I'd been through many sudden, rug-ripped-out changes, but this one was different. My sister had been there through all the other sudden changes, and we'd just started to really grow close, but suddenly I was on my own. It was a paradigm shift of moving from being the invisible middle child to the oldest in a split second. All of a sudden, my sister, my buffer, my steady protector, was gone.

Talk about a pity party. I was not quite thirteen years old, and there I was, the one with the unrealistic expectations of our mother. I had my eight-year-old brother to care for, who was afraid of the dark, while I had my own terrors of the dark; my mom was at work all the time, and my older sister, who I didn't think was afraid of anything, was gone.

I had many moments of just feeling truly disassociated in that void. I don't know how often it happened, but I had deep experiences of dissociation. I remember one time lying in the living room on the floor, staring at the ceiling, feeling completely paralyzed. It was the same paralysis that happened as a small girl when my stepfather came to me in my sleep and climbed into my bed to violate my young body. I was unable to move and barely able to breathe.

Jeffrey was screaming my name, over and over, and was shaking me. I could hear him, but I was a thousand miles away. I don't know why I was on the floor. I don't know if I hadn't had any alcohol or drugs that day. I think it was just an experience of complete overwhelm and shutdown that led to a serious dis-sociative moment. I don't know where I'd gone, but when I came to, my very frightened little brother was hovering over me, cry-ing, completely terrified that I had died.

I hugged him, and he hugged me, and we just cried. "I thought you were dead," he said.

"I'm right here. I'm okay," I replied through my own tears. I felt like he saved me in that moment, but from what, I'm not quite sure.

In that moment, I questioned whether I *had* died because I couldn't see, hear, or feel anything. I was completely and utterly disconnected in every sense of the word. I'd disconnected/dis-associated in this same way before, but not to a degree where I had such a hard time snapping out of it. While it was scary, it also had a sense of peace to it. It made the idea of death appealing.

It was a very difficult transition when Lorri left, but my grandmother came to stay with us sometimes. She would cook, clean, and tell us what to do. I had a reprieve from the overwhelm of trying to understand the degree of responsibility that had just escalated a few flights up. I had that familiar security when she was there, but it wasn't steady. I knew that she'd be going back to Carmen's in a day or two and that Jeff and I would be on our own again. I learned to show a strong front when she left, but the little girl in me just wanted my grandma.

Luckily, I was offered a job at a restaurant where my aunt Debbie and uncle Renee managed the kitchen. They offered my cousin Mike and me jobs to wash dishes, prep-cook, host, and bus tables on weekends and even on school nights when we could get there. Mom liked the idea too and agreed to make sure Jeffrey would be taken care of when I worked. This was a much-needed reprieve from the responsibilities of managing a child and a home, for both the jovial atmosphere of the restaurant and the opportunity to make money.

From as young as I can remember, one of the chains I'd dreamed about breaking was the struggle with money. We heard "we can't afford it" as a regular cadence. We rarely wore what the other kids wore or participated in sports, so this was a new and exciting shift. The escape to the restaurant and the possibility of good tips became another escape, as I worked every chance I could. It led to a sense of control in my life that allowed me to not only buy a few things that made me feel like I fit in, but it also allowed me to join several of my friends who had gotten into roller skating.

Izzy was a close friend who lived in the townhome behind ours. She and I would always take Jeffrey to the roller rink. We didn't always stay at the rink, as we hung out with some older kids who would sneak out of session and go drink or smoke pot. I also met Cheri and found a kindred spirit in that she, too, had struggled with her single mom and home life.

The year after Lorri left came with a lot of change. I started working, began speed-skating competitively, and we moved and changed schools twice. I was used to a lot of change, and while the job and skating were both things I feel I needed, this new chapter of life without Lorri was chaotic and extremely stressful. I so badly wanted to be a good kid and avoid going through what my sister had, but at thirteen years old, every day felt like a tornado of school, housework, managing my younger brother, managing my own interests with work and skating, and managing my mother's emotions on the nights she came home drunk at three a.m. ranting about the house or her boyfriend or some customer that didn't leave a tip that night.

I'd stepped into the role of being the eldest child, and often the adult, and my mother had no hesitation in reminding me of this on a regular basis.

"You're the oldest now," or "You should know better," were familiar lines that I hated. I didn't want to be the oldest, and I didn't want to have the responsibilities that had been thrust upon me. I wanted to be a kid, and the pressure caused a lot of frustration, so I took out a lot of the anger I felt about that on Jeffrey.

I wasn't good at being the version of a big sister who made him do homework or eat dinner. If he didn't do what I told him, I would chase him and either hit him or put him in a closet and hold the door closed. But as soon as I heard his terrified screams, I opened the door and apologized profusely.

It was like I had this dual personality, and I didn't know either person.

I would promise never to do it again, and until he got old enough to fight back, I kept breaking that promise. To this day, I feel guilty for how I hurt, scared, and abused him.

He was craving attention and connection, too. So, part of this vicious cycle was that he would say no or be defiant intentionally. As I understand it now, it was a way to have these intense emotional exchanges because we weren't playing cards or sitting next to each other watching a show anymore. On the nights we skated, I'd abandon him at the rink to fend for himself. And if I wasn't at work, I had dishes to do, dinner to cook, boxes to unpack, and homework. So, the whole apple cart was tumbled, and it wasn't a very sturdy apple cart to begin with.

I have no idea how we didn't kill each other or burn the house down in the times when my mother or grandmother weren't there, which was far too often. We were highly unsupervised kids, and most of my choices were those of someone too young to be in charge of such responsibilities. So, under that degree of pressure, stress, and sheer immaturity, I made *many* mistakes.

Mistakes always caused a shouting match with my mother. We were not actually in the house at the same time a lot, so she didn't really have a clue how many plates I was spinning. And when she was home and something wasn't as she'd expected, a big fight would break out. One of the worst fights we'd ever had was shortly after I'd turned thirteen and had started to fight back.

She was getting ready to leave for a doctor's appointment when the fight escalated into a screaming match.

"You better have the kitchen cleaned *right* by the time I get back."

"If you ever come back home," I replied sarcastically as I was angry about how often she was gone. "I'm not supposed to be the mother of a nine-year-old boy and have to clean up after him, you, and everyone!"

"I don't want to hear it. You have a nice home, are in a good school, and I work my ass off for you to have that," she gaslighted. Then added some name-calling: "Ingrate."

I rolled my eyes. "I do everything, Mom! I grocery shop. I clean. I go to school. I have a freaking job! I take care of Jeff. And where are you? Not here!"

Part of me just wanted my mom to be home; the other part just wanted to be let off the hook from all of the pressure.

We'd gone back and forth and had been yelling at each other for about twenty minutes or more, and we were both just exasperated. I had spent a year in extreme stress, and she'd spent our entire lives trying to get away from us. We had both pretty much lost it, and then there was the final blow.

"You're just like your sister!" she yelled in my face as she slammed the door and left the house.

The emotions were at a tipping point, and these words hit like a sledgehammer. I knew how badly broken my sister and mother's relationship was, and I had been pretty broken just witnessing it. If I were just like my sister, I would be just as disposable to my mother as my sister was. Living anywhere but with my mother, even though I had such deep resentment, felt scary as hell. I knew I had nowhere to go.

I was home alone and spent probably thirty minutes walking around in a circle in the downstairs of our townhome, vacillating among anger, fear, and deep hurt. My sister had lied a lot and gotten caught stealing money from my mom, sneaking out, sneaking friends in, and a variety of other things that they had fought about before she left.

I walked the circle around the bathroom, into the living room, then the kitchen, then the hallway back to the living room again. "I'm nothing like her!" I shouted at the walls.

I hadn't done any of that at this point. I had decent grades. I worked. I found a sport I liked and dedicated myself to the training as often as I could. I took care of my brother and the house, maybe not perfectly, but I was there. I cried and cursed, still walking. I was vacillating between yelling and talking to myself and my absent mother: "Why do you hate her so much? Where am I going to go? What am I going to do? Who will take care of Jeff if you kick me out, too?"

I was sure that getting kicked out was coming.

A feeling of defeat, hopelessness, and just being unable to get anything right turned into not wanting to exist, which became a serious option as the minutes went by.

I just wanted the struggle to end, the ranting, the memories, the overwhelm, and the sheer feeling of being completely irrelevant.

I went upstairs to my mother's bathroom, grabbed one of her many prescriptions, and took it downstairs to the kitchen. I looked at it for several minutes with tears just streaming down my face. I dumped it out on the counter and counted the number of pills. There were nineteen. I felt such a deep sense of disconnect and aloneness with no way out, and in an impulsive moment, those pills became my solution. I got a glass of water and swallowed every pill.

A few minutes passed, and I didn't feel anything. I realized that I had no idea what kind of pill I'd taken, so I had no idea how it would affect me.

I called 411 and got the number for Suicide Prevention. I dialed the number and hung up. "Fuck it," I said as I threw the phone and sat on the floor in the hallway. I didn't care how I would die.

But the curiosity came again. I started to feel antsy, so I called the hotline back and asked the woman on the other end what kind of effect the pills I had taken would have on "someone." I wanted to know how I was going to die. The kind lady explained that the pills were a form of speed and that if *someone* took too many of them, their heart could go crazy and possibly just stop. She also gently explained that *someone* might survive it, using my own words. She said that if the person survived, it could cause severe damage to their heart or nervous system.

I just got quiet. I didn't want to say it out loud that I'd already taken the pills. I had tears streaming down my face and just wanted to sob.

"Honey, did you take these pills?"

It took me a minute to compose myself and breathe enough to answer, but I managed to say yes.

I don't know what she said next that convinced me to give her my address, but I started crying audibly and begged her to ask the emergency responders not to come with sirens. I don't know why that mattered to me as much, other than the fact that I was conditioned not to want to be embarrassed by onlooking neighbors.

She kept talking to me, asking questions about the color of my shirt and whether it was my favorite color. It was a Journey T-shirt, and I told her how much I loved their music. She loved them too and just kept me talking about their music and the lead singer, Steve Perry.

It was about five to ten minutes of her keeping me talking when I heard sirens at a distance, and then I heard them stop about a block away. I knew they were there for me.

"I can hear them," I said. "Thank you for asking them to turn off the sirens."

"You're welcome, Sweetheart. Are they at the door yet?"

I went to open the door, and I saw several firemen and paramedics walking up the sidewalk of our complex. "They're here."

The first paramedic walked up to me and asked, "Are you Paula?"

"Yes," I said, feeling a deep sense of shame and embarrassment that they had to come help me. He took the phone to assure the kind lady that they were there, and two other paramedics and a fireman swiftly walked me over to the sofa to check my vitals. They gave me some ipecac syrup and explained this would make me vomit, but they couldn't assure me that the drugs wouldn't have a severe effect, so we needed to get to a hospital. They were walking me out to the ambulance when my mother arrived back home with a very concerned look on her face.

I immediately broke down in tears.

"I'm so sorry. I'm so sorry," I kept saying. The taller fireman who was standing there put his arm around my shoulder, and I just buried my face into his chest. I had no idea who he was or what to do, but I was eternally grateful for that gesture in that moment.

Two of the paramedics explained what had happened, and my mother asked if she could take me to the hospital herself. She handed me a small trash can, and we drove to the hospital. I threw up twice on the way.

The ER was chaos and humiliation. I remember getting an IV and having to roll the pole the bag was hanging from to the bathroom to vomit a few times. There was a steady stream of different doctors, nurses, and even a police officer in and out of the ER bay asking the same thousand questions over and over about me, about our fight, about our home life. It was a rude awakening to see the different responses each person had to the circumstances in which I was there. Some were very compassionate and were obviously in a role that they took to heart dearly. Others had a look of disgust or just apathy as they checked the monitors or asked questions. It was a horrible feeling to consider that I'd wasted someone's time. My intuitive nature felt their judgment that I was there just to get attention and that it was my mother's fault I'd gone to such an extreme measure to get through to her.

I did truly consider whether the energy I was picking up was accurate. Was this nothing more than an attempt to get attention? I rolled that thought around in my head along with the eight million others that were racing as rapidly as my heart rate. The drugs had definitely kicked in. Everything felt so heightened, and I was visibly shaking.

My mother was distraught, but present and answering every question while she stood next to the gurney I was on. They checked my eyes and heart every few minutes and eventually sent us home. I couldn't tell you what time we arrived or the time we left, but it was dark when we finally drove home.

After I was released, my mother cried on the way home. She was blaming herself just as much as I was blaming myself. I don't remember much about the conversation, as I struggled to focus on the words and the lights on the streets, which seemed too sharp and bright. The best way I can describe how I felt is to say that my skin was crawling.

Writhing with a heightened awareness and unable to get comfortable, I squirmed in the front seat. I was emotionally wrought with conflict. I was so relieved to be going home and that my mother was by my side. Yet, hours before, I was fully intent on ending my life.

I was awake for three days straight, and my mother never left the house once. The idea of my young life ending scared us both terribly. On that third day, I fell asleep around noon. When I woke and realized I'd slept, I stood up and called to my mom, "Mom! I slept for four hours!"

However, I stood up too quickly and fainted in the hallway. I remember getting dizzy and everything going black, and the next thing I knew, I was screaming and throwing punches, fighting with complete rage at my mother on the hallway floor as she was trying to get me to realize I was safe.

I don't know if I was aware that it was her and I was angry, or if I was just in a state of terror and entirely incoherent from the damage of the drugs, but when I did realize it was her, I started crying and let her hold me. She rocked me in the hall-way, and I let her. I needed her, and for those few minutes together, she needed me, too.

I would like to tell you that the relationship with my mother was forever changed by this incident, but unfortunately, that is not the case. There will always be a special place in my heart and memory for how she handled this, and even a few other events in the lives of my siblings and mine. But the familiar is comfortable. Our familiar was disconnected, detached, and dys-functional. So, while she handled this situation beautifully, handling the majority of life chaotically was the norm.

Gratefully, I never considered suicide seriously again. The thought came. Defeat and hopelessness came, too, but the memories of those moments at the front door when she walked in, and in the hall where she rocked me, even after I'd swung at her repeatedly, were stronger. Additionally, the knowledge that I'd damaged my nervous system was always present. The knowledge that trying and failing could make life worse was al-ways present. This experience wasn't enough for me to stop finding ways to alter my state with drugs and alcohol, but it was enough for me to more sincerely cradle and care for my dream of breaking the chain and building a better life.

CHAPTER 6
The Seed Was Planted

"SOMETIMES WHEN YOU ARE IN A DARK PLACE, YOU FEEL THAT
YOU'VE BEEN BURIED, WHEN IN FACT YOU'VE BEEN PLANTED."
~ CHRISTINE CAINE

IT WAS A THURSDAY, and it was my fifteenth birthday. I'd taken the city bus straight from school to pick up a few hours of work at the restaurant, as I knew tips were often better on holidays and birthdays. I also knew it would be a quick shift, and I could sneak in a few birthday swigs while there. I'd often snuck in the last few sips of a customer's drinks that they hadn't finished. I was disgusted with myself for this habit, but it was free and easy to get a buzz.

My grandmother was at our house with my brother, so I asked if I could stay at Izzy's after work and go to school from there the next day. Since it was my birthday, and I'd often stayed at Izzy's, there was no protest.

Izzy and her mom had moved to an apartment a few blocks away and were on the same bus line as my house, so when I took the city bus, I often got off a stop earlier to go hang out there. I got there around nine p.m. and let myself in. "Hi Honey, I'm home!" I shouted jokingly over the music.

Izzy jumped up and came to hug me. "Happy Birthday!" she said, grabbing my hand and walking me into her bedroom. There were a few friends there when I arrived, and two of them stood up to leave as it was a school night and they had to get home. We smiled cordially, and as they put on their shoes, I took mine off.

"I'm Shannon," said one of the girls Izzy had become good friends with, as Izzy walked the other two out. "I don't have to be home tonight," she said with a bit of a sly grin, and she added, "Happy Birthday," and handed me the half-empty bottle of cheap rum they'd been drinking. I took the bottle, tipped it for a swig, smiled, and sat on the floor beside her.

Izzy came back in and asked if I was hungry. "Duh," I said, as I was always hungry. I was stick thin and ate more than anyone I knew. I loved to eat, and Izzy loved to make me feel at home.

Izzy and her mother had a two-bedroom apartment, and I was there all the time. She was a year younger, so we had some different friends, but she and her mother, Colette, felt like family to me. Colette was very accepting of our "teenageism" and always treated me like I was her own daughter. She was our most frequent ride to the skating rink, and when my brother wasn't around, she would smoke pot with us. She laughed with us (and *at* us), and sometimes shared wonderful words of wisdom. We loved her. It was a place where I loved being, and Izzy was someone I cherished like a sister.

Izzy was in the kitchen, and as Shannon and I started to talk and laugh, we became fast friends. If you'd asked me how long I'd known her, I would have instinctively said, "My entire life." This natural soulmate bond of friendship was immediate, and even better in this hazy stage of my life, she instinctively and immediately became a new partner in crime.

Izzy came back with some macaroni and cheese and a bag of chips, and we all ate, drank what was left of the rum with a soda we were sharing, and sat up until the early morning hours talking, listening to music, laughing, and most of all, trying to be quiet so we didn't wake Colette. We didn't have enough alcohol to get really drunk that night, and in reflection, I think that was Divine Intervention. We connected with one another on a deep level instead.

My favorite part of the night was meeting Shannon. She was Izzy's friend first and foremost, and I truly respected that, but even Izzy felt the connection Shannon and I had made. She laughingly commented, "You got a best friend for your birthday!"

We were often at Izzy's because Colette liked knowing where we were and knowing we were not running wild somewhere else. She understood our rebellious nature and need to individuate. She knew the five of us who ran together the most—Bonnie, Shannon, Cheri, Izzy, and me—all were a bit wild, but she had a fond memory of her own teenage years, so she didn't shame us or lecture us too often. She reminded us to be safe and stay together if we went out.

Ages fifteen to seventeen were a bit of a blur. Jeffrey became old enough to stay home or go to the rink without me. Lorri moved in with a new boyfriend, so I enjoyed spending more time with her away from the typical family gatherings. She and her new beau sold pot, so I had the bonus of always having marijuana. It was the eighties, and my small circle of friends and fellow speed skaters went to rock concerts and parties and hitch-hiked everywhere.

Shannon and I became inseparable and took pride in being wilder and more reckless than the others. Upon reflection, it wasn't really about the level of wild; it was a stronger avoidance of our home lives. Shannon and I would do anything to avoid being at our own homes, and equally, just about anything to hang out together. We were often up until all hours of the morning talking, and on many occasions, we never slept at all. We used to get the biggest kick out of the fact that we would often show up wearing the same color or style. It was something that everyone noticed, and it was never planned. We were just very kindred soul-sisters, and it became known that our bond was very close.

We didn't care how insane some of our ideas sounded. As long as we were together, we would be okay. We lied to every adult in our lives and often even lied to Colette about the risky situations we'd put ourselves in.

After school one day, I was at Izzy's when Shannon showed up, and I could tell she'd been crying. She had this look of defeat and fear on her face, and it took her a minute to get her head around what had just happened enough to tell us.

Her mother had totally destroyed her room. She had torn all her posters off the wall, drained her waterbed, and cut the mattress down the middle. All her clothes and other things were piled in the middle of her bedroom floor, and her mother just repeatedly screamed at her, "Get out!" She said she couldn't take anything with her, and just to get out. Her mother had clearly lost her temper, and Shannon was in shock.

Shannon's mother had learned that Shannon had been ditching classes. Her parents already knew that Shannon was smoking, drinking, and had tried many drugs, so this was the last straw, and her mother truly lost it.

Shannon stayed at Izzy's, Bonnie's, at my house, and floated from friend to friend for a while, drinking even more, drugging even more, pushing the wild and reckless a bit more. Within a few weeks, her parents, who obviously didn't really want her to leave but to conform to their wishes, found her.

Izzy, Cheri, and I were about to walk to Izzy's from school when Izzy gave us the news. "Shannon's parents put her in rehab."

I remember thinking that this felt way too radical. I was invincible in my own mind and believed Shannon was, too. I completely disagreed with the idea that she needed any rehabilitation from drugs. I sincerely felt this was an extreme overreaction and, even more so, an act of punishment. I was so flippant about it and made fun of the situation often.

One night, probably three weeks later, Shannon called me at home from a phone in a church hallway. I remember being so very excited to hear her voice, as I'd been worried and missed her terribly. I asked her how it was, and she said she was happy she was there. She told me that she was at a church where a twelve-step meeting was held and that she really liked the people.

In less than a split second, my entire view on the situation changed. I knew her voice and tone well, and she was sincere. We were very soul-connected, and I was happy if she was happy. It was simple. Every opinion I'd had on the matter shifted instantly. I suddenly wanted to find this church to see what this smile in her voice was all about. I knew something was good, and I wanted to share that with her.

"So, tell me more," I inquired.

"I can only talk for a second, because I'm not allowed to be talking to you," she laughed.

I laughed too, because I thought she was joking.

"My parents made me sign this stupid contract stating I would never speak to you again."

"Seriously?!" I replied in disbelief, wondering if they could even do that.

"Yes!" She replied and started laughing. "Whatever, they're idiots."

We both laughed loudly together because we knew there was no way this would ever be honored. We trusted our bond and connection, so it was truly humorous to consider that they felt they could keep us apart.

For the next few weeks, I went about my typical behavior of working and sneaking drinks. I also stole bottles of alcohol from the restaurant so I could drink more. Skating turned from being a decent form of athleticism to a crazy ride of being overly wild on the floor with Cheri and sneaking out more frequently with the older kids to have sex in cars and get loaded.

My friendship with Shannon had been a shining light of acceptance and connection unlike any of the others, and I struggled to cope in her absence. I truly loved Izzy, Cheri, and Bonnie, and I leaned on them, but when it came to Shannon's absence, I began avoiding any semblance of emotion. Reckless amounts of drinking, lack of sleep, and any chance of escapism I could find escalated, and I invited anyone along who was willing to allow my lousy influence to join in. Cheri and I were absolutely out of control at the skating rink, recklessly racing through the crowds with extreme adrenaline, and then getting kicked off the floor and grabbing Izzy to leave the rink and go party with the older teens with cars.

Since Cheri had a similar home life to mine, I leaned into our friendship and was grateful for the bond we shared. Similar to Izzy's, Bonnie's parents had always welcomed all of us. I floated from friend's home to friend's home and sometimes landed at Lorri's place. I rarely went home but for a change of clothes.

I had this very clear, yet very teenage and immature notion that when Shannon got out, everything would be back to normal between us. She would join in with the wild and reckless behavior just as before, and all would be set right again.

After she got out of rehab, she would sneak phone calls to me, and we would see each other at school. She declined every hit of pot or offer for alcohol after rehab. She was being drug tested, so she was really on the up and up. Even then, with her own clear answer to say no, I believed that it would be any minute before she'd "be back to normal." In all of my haze of substance use and alteration, I simply couldn't wrap my head around this version of her.

She got a job at an ice cream shop and told me her schedule so I could come see her without consequence. She didn't plan to honor the written contract, but didn't want her parents to know that we were still talking, to which I fully agreed. I didn't want anything to do with them or risk causing her more trouble.

However, I didn't quite understand what it meant to respect her choice to say no when it came to any of the drugs or alcohol we were doing without her. I thought it was all a show to pass the drug tests.

I'll never forget the day that I pulled into the parking lot of the ice cream shop and took a huge hit off my pot pipe in the car. I held my breath and ran into the shop, right up next to her behind the counter, and blew the smoke on her so she could smell it. We had both loved the smell, so I had this idea that she could smell it without getting high, and I'd be doing her some kind of favor.

She laughed, and then I saw the look on her face shift to "Well, shit."

Lo and behold, I'd just happened to choose to run in and blow pot smoke at her when her mother was also in the shop! And she saw the whole thing. Her mother's look of pure disgust and even hatred was palpable. But based on the many unkind things she'd said and done to Shannon over the time we'd been friends, my feelings for her were mutual, so I laughed it off. We both did.

We both knew I needed to leave fast. She hugged me quickly, but very tightly, and said, "Love you."

"Love you," I replied as I hurried out the door.

Not long after that, Shannon informed us that she and her family would be leaving Colorado and moving to New Mexico at the end of the school year. Although she was angry about it and didn't want to go, she was also clearheaded and knew she had no other option.

The same week that Shannon told us she was moving to New Mexico, my mother told me that we would also be moving again. We had lived in this particular area for almost three years. There had been two different homes, but in the same area. It was the longest we'd ever lived in the same area and gone to the same schools.

This move would have meant my thirteenth school transfer, and I was unwilling to switch schools again. I was seventeen years old, in the middle of my junior year of high school, and I told Shannon that I couldn't switch schools again and that I was going to drop out. Our bond was so connected that my solution became hers, too.

We both knew that this era of our lives was over. So, being the soul-bonded friends that we were, we chose to drop out together.

We walked through the building together, facing each teacher who had to sign off on the document requiring us to terminate our high school experience.

It was a bittersweet day. Part of me felt deeply justified, and I was grateful I wasn't alone. Another part of me felt extreme failure and guilt, not only for giving up but also for feeling like I'd influenced Shannon.

She assured me that she would have made this choice with or without me and given our fierce loyalty to one another, I believed that at the time. I question it now, of course, but then, with that level of maturity and despair, I accepted it as truth.

Shortly after dropping out and Shannon moving away, I drifted into a deeper degree of not only disconnect, but wild and reckless escapism. I was losing my high school diploma and my best friend. It was another feeling of the rug being ripped out from under me, and I knew that meant haunting memories, impossible emotions, and hurt. All things I ran hard from.

By this time, my grandmother wasn't at our house as often, and I felt a lot of shame for my behavior around her, so I was distancing myself. None of us were skating anymore, either. It just seemed to fizzle out. I was disconnecting from my friends, brother, grandmother, any sense of direction, and myself.

I started a new job waiting tables at a diner and began drinking more heavily every day. I was introduced to other people in that job who did a lot of cocaine and who were connected to a drug dealer, who allowed me to stay at his place often. It was a deeper dive into the shadows of alcoholism and drug addiction. I became a complete garbage can and would take nearly any drug put in front of me. The only limit was intravenous drugs.

I did cocaine, acid, and what was called "crank" at the time, but was actually meth. I drank mostly whiskey as I had a fake ID by then and could buy booze at liquor stores or any bar and drink anything I wanted.

I had my driver's license too, so I drove my mother's car rather often and drove drunk far too many times.

The blackouts continued, and the hangovers started to become notable. I'd had them in my earlier teen years, but they became more difficult as I was pushing this daily envelope of destruction.

And I couldn't stop.

I could see the impending train wreck. I knew the pace that had quickened wasn't good, but every morning when I woke up sick, aching everywhere, nauseous, and ashamed, I knew that I'd probably do it again that same night.

I'd considered what Shannon may have found in her new path of sobriety. I'd thought about whether I could ever stop or even if I needed rehab myself, and that's as far as it went: a brief consideration. One that I had every day, but regardless, it was brief. I was lost in life. I was missing my friend and felt the deepening of the disconnect I'd known too well. I stayed at Izzy's for a while, and we did the same thing we'd always done, except she got up and went to school. I'd be left alone in her apartment until I went to work for a lunch or dinner shift at the diner, and it all just felt empty.

My mother and I were in our familiar power struggle. I would take the car and disappear until the next morning. And then I'd blame her and gaslight her for my behavior, saying I learned it from her. Jeffrey spent a lot of time alone now and was venturing down his own path as a teen. Nothing was the same, and I was just truly baffled about my next steps in life.

Shannon came to mind often. In some of the worst next-morning moments of hangover sickness and shame, I'd wonder what her life was like. I wondered if I'd ever see her again.

I loved and admired her every move, and even though I was older, which holds a lot of clout when you're a teen, I felt she was way ahead of me in life. It was both a loss and a gain. She wasn't there physically with us any longer, but my ability to imagine her new life clean and sober made me proud of her. It planted a seed of what it may be like to live better, think better, feel better, and perhaps be welcomed back into her life rather than contractually exiled.

The impact of this period of my life was significant. The disconnect and deepening into my alcoholism were dark and damaging. The friendship with Shannon and then the loss of her was deeply conflicting and confusing. The independence to choose for myself about dropping out, and yet having no direction or next steps, left me just feeling lost.

However, there was that seed... That place buried deep that had some semblance of belief that light may just be out there.

CHAPTER 7
Lost in the Wilderness

"WHEN EVERYTHING SEEMS TO BE GOING AGAINST YOU, REMEMBER THAT THE AIRPLANE TAKES OFF AGAINST THE WIND, NOT WITH IT."
~ HENRY FORD

I DON'T KNOW WHAT DAY IT WAS. I woke up in the basement at my mother's newest residence. She'd moved into a townhome, and it had a finished basement with rust colored shag carpet. The color alone made me a little nauseous, but the hangover was the real issue. The pain in my head and body was severe. I felt like I'd been poisoned, and since I'm being honest about what alcoholism is, I had been.

I could barely move and all I wanted to do was close my eyes again, but it was nine a.m., and I had to be at work by ten. As I came to, the realization hit me that I was at my mom's house, but I'd told her I was staying at Izzy's. I don't remember how I got there, but I knew that I'd left there the day before in her car.

Then a panicked thought set in. *"Oh my God, did I drive?"*

If anyone knew how drunk I got regularly, it was me. I knew that my drunken behavior was that of stumbling, slurring, and often ranting about some injustice, or crying about my sad life.

I never remembered specifics, but it was always humiliating to consider even the very few memories of the night before.

Fear rushed over me, triggering a surge of adrenaline. If I did drive, I didn't drive well. I could have hurt someone. I started scanning the basement for the car keys and saw them on the floor, lying next to my purse with other things that had fallen out.

The townhome had a carport with two parking spaces in the back. As I opened the back door, I saw the car parked almost between the lines, but definitely not parked well. I was so upset with myself that I'd chosen to drive home, and I didn't remember any of it.

This wasn't the first time I'd done this, but every time I did, I had this terrible fear that I'd hurt someone. So, I walked outside barefoot and around the car to see if there were any dents. In my mind, it wasn't really dents that I was looking for; it was any sign that I'd hit a person or animal. I imagined seeing blood or torn clothing on a bumper or on the grill. It was such a horrible feeling of shame and disbelief.

"Why do I do this? What is wrong with me? Paula, you're an idiot!" I would literally say these things out loud.

I am grateful that there was never any sign of damage to the car or anything (anyone) else, but I am humiliated to say that it wasn't the last time I'd "walked the car."

Every time I drank enough to get drunk, which was too frequently, blackouts happened. I'd wake up the next day with few, if any, memories from the night before. In the early years of my minimally supervised teenage life, marked by poor choices, I would recall a moment or two of laughter and silliness as a couple of friends and I, who had snuck out in the middle of the night, walked in the dark and disturbed the peace. But as the volume of these experiences increased, the hints of memory became equally as unsettling as the memories I was trying to bury from my earlier life.

I would wake up in places and not know how I got there. Some memories were all too unbecoming of a young lady. I had been in strange places with strange people, conducting lewd acts. And in those many nights, I had very little concern for anything other than getting more alcohol or drugs and getting more and more wasted.

I dreaded hearing the stories of my behavior. In my early teen years, I was told that I was funny and that the crazy choices we had made were my ideas. I would pretend to laugh it off, but I was always embarrassed. In my older teens, the stories from the nights before became darker. I would remember so little and would dread asking anyone who was with me what I had done.

I'd remember being angry, yelling, or throwing things, but I had no idea what had upset me. I'd remember getting in someone's face to fight, and people would pull me back and often laugh at me.

The one time I got in an actual fight, it was Shannon's face that I'll never forget.

She was either in town from New Mexico visiting family or went to see Izzy under the false premise that I would not be there. Her parents allowed her to visit Izzy because they knew Colette was typically there, and just having a parent present made it allowable.

When she came over, she was very clear that she had no intention of drinking, but we were on our way to an outdoor party in a hidden field, and she didn't have much choice but to join us. Again, I'll add that in my own state of delusion about her sobriety and clean living, I still didn't truly believe she had taken any of it seriously. I hadn't known any other version of Shannon but the one I'd partied with, and because of both my low level of maturity and out-of-control behavior, I just couldn't make sense of this version of her at that time. I'd missed her presence in the party scene, too, so, selfishly, I really wanted to have a feeling of reunion.

When we arrived at the field, there were at least fifty people there. There was a keg, and my first stop was to get a beer. I began drinking and just floating around the field a bit with Shannon, Izzy, and Bonnie when Brook arrived.

Brook had been my nemesis because she had hurt Izzy's feelings a few years earlier, and my fierce protective nature used that as justification to become a very mean and hateful person to her.

Those who knew we were enemies had been hearing the things both Brook and I had said about each other over the last few months, so they began to egg me on to fight her. They'd heard us both talk about kicking the other's ass several times by then. Add in a keg, several drunken teens, and the sun setting, and well, it's easy to imagine the setup.

I didn't want to fight at all, as I wanted to spend time with Shannon, but I also feared embarrassment if I didn't confront her. I'd also slammed at least two or three full beers by then, so while I was lucid, I wasn't sober.

The egging on continued, Brook and I made eye contact, and that was it. I had to decide what I would do. So, I walked up to her.

"I hear you've been talking some shit about me," I said, trying to look and sound tough as an audience began to form.

"I haven't said anything about you," she replied, looking a bit intimidated, which I intended.

"I don't believe you," I said. "Who here heard her say she wants to kick my ass?"

And that's all it took.

A chant started. "Fight! Fight! Fight!"

So, I swung and hit her in the face with my fist, and she quickly put me in a headlock and socked me in the right temple at least five times, hard, before I got her to the ground and was crouched on top of her, banging the back of her head on the dirt field.

She had somehow gotten her leg around me and pushed me to my feet while she was still sitting on the ground, and the crowd was going crazy. "Kick her in the head!" one girl shouted. I was hurt and had never been in a fight with anyone but my siblings. I didn't really know what to do, but I knew I didn't want to kick someone sitting on the ground.

I yelled at her to get up, while sincerely hoping that she wouldn't.

We'd had all of a one-to-two-minute fight and were both shaken to the core. "If you don't get up, then you know this means I kicked your ass!" I yelled and I waited.

The crowd kept yelling, and all she said was, "I'm not getting up. I'm not fighting you anymore."

I turned around to walk away and saw Shannon's face. It was a look of complete horror and utter disappointment. Brook was not someone she hated alongside me—she was her friend, and I'd intended to hurt her.

Shannon had likely seen me drunk and angry before, but she had never seen me rage. And this one I couldn't hide from with any excuse of not remembering. I hadn't had that much to drink yet. I was lucid enough to vividly remember this moment. I felt like I had completely let Shannon down, and I was ashamed.

I could feel the pounding of my eye that Brook had socked numerous times. I don't even know if Brook was hurt, and if so, how bad, but I knew she'd gotten the better of me.

Shannon and Izzy left together. I saw Brook across the field leaving, too. Bonnie and I stayed and drank more, and the rest of that night was a blur as I reached that familiar state of serious intoxication.

I woke up the next morning with a pretty severe black eye. On the top and bottom of my eye formed a perfect black and purple circle, and I truly felt I'd deserved it.

Shannon and I talked briefly about it, and she was forgiving as usual, but I didn't know what to say except that I was sorry. I truly was—for Brook, for Shannon, for the whole situation.

During this period of deeper decline into alcoholism, I remember the look on many people's faces who were frustrated or disgusted with me, or often just embarrassed to be seen with me. The next-day conversations with those I'd partied with the night before were cringeworthy for all of us when I had to ask what I'd done. Telling someone they'd made a complete fool of themselves, even if they asked to know, was difficult.

As these moments of humiliation, confusion, and shame began to add up, so did my awareness that I was an alcoholic. I had grown up around alcoholism my entire life, and it was not lost on me what this condition looked like. I knew that the instant the alcohol began to take effect, my personality was going to change. I knew that I would say things I would never say sober. I knew that I would behave in ways that were not only inappropriate but embarrassing. I knew that my wounds of abuse, abandonment, and neglect would lead to many sexual encounters in an effort to fill a void that would become an even more bottomless pit every time I followed through on the various engagements any drunken night would offer. I also knew that I would take more risks and engage in behavior that could get me injured, in legal trouble, or even killed. And yet, I would jump at every chance I could to drink or use a mind-altering substance in search of that inebriated haze that was so seductive to my wounded soul.

The awareness of my bloodline began to haunt me. I knew what I had inherited. The many moments of sitting by a window as a child and dreaming of how much better I would be when I grew up were becoming a stab wound to my heart. I was letting myself down, and I knew it. I had this deep desire to change my trajectory and grow up to be different, but at only fourteen years old, I suspected I was an alcoholic. At age sixteen, I knew I was in trouble. By age eighteen, I had no hesitation in my conscience that I had an insidious condition that was ruling my life.

In my delusion and denial, I believed that if I just kept "practicing," I would outgrow the blackouts and be better able to handle alcohol. I had a tough time reconciling the fact that they kept getting worse with the fact that I was only a teenager. I knew that I had a problem, and in certain moments of clarity, I also knew that the solution was *not drinking*. However, these moments of clarity were sparse.

It was just like I'd seen in many cartoons or TV programs. I had an angel on one shoulder and a devil on the other. The angel would be hopeful and humble, giving me the energy that there was a different life for me. The angel would remind me that I wanted to be a good person and that I wanted more for my life than the path I was walking. I felt the words and emotions of how I could be healthy, clearheaded, and even wise.

Then there was the devil. This leather-clad cool chick had a cigarette in one hand, a drink in the other, dark sunglasses, and this invincible energy that made me delusionally believe that I wasn't as bad as all of the other alcoholics in the world, especially the many of them I'd known in my family.

There were countless mornings when I would wake up sick, tired, humiliated, and completely confused, and in an effort *not* to feel any of that, the disconnect would just deepen.

One morning I woke up next to a man I had flirted with the night before. I was eighteen and he was probably in his twenties. I was lying there with my hangover headache, body aches, and nausea, trying to remember his name. I had no idea how we had gotten to his house. I didn't even know if the place we were in was his.

I quietly got out of bed in hopes of not waking him. I got dressed, sick to my stomach from both the hangover and sheer disgust. I may not have remembered his name, but I was sure about what had happened in that bed.

I wandered into the small house and saw some mail on the counter. I shuffled through it to try to find the address of where I was. I found a few pieces with different names, none that I recognized, and the same address, and I quietly walked outside to compare the number on the house to the number on the items of mail. I set the mail back as I'd found it and left.

As I had done for many years, I started walking. It was daylight, and I knew the city incredibly well. Denver has a straight-forward street grid that is easy to follow, so anyone who knows it can figure out where they are in the city. I'm not sure how or why I learned this so young, but I knew how to find my way around town on foot, by bus, in a car, but most of all by hitch-hiking.

I was not in the best part of town. It was a high-crime area, and I was nervous to put my thumb out. However, I was wearing a pair of very high-heeled boots and knew that I had two options. I had to walk back into that house, ask that stranger his name, and then ask for a ride home, or I had to put out my thumb and ask a different stranger in a scary neighborhood for a ride. I chose the latter, and I never saw that man again.

There were so many moments of awareness that I was following in the footsteps of those whom I resented and had such disregard and disrespect for. Yet, I was so lost in the wilderness of disconnect that I truly had no idea what to do to stop the cycle. It was like there would be a daily awakening that I should do better. Then, the shame and overwhelm of having no idea how to stop would continue. I'd keep disconnecting from the disconnect and running into oblivion.

CHAPTER 8

Shotgun Willie's

"YOUR LIFE CHANGES THE MOMENT YOU MAKE A NEW,
CONGRUENT, AND COMMITTED DECISION."
~ TONY ROBBINS

DURING MY YEARS OF ILLEGAL and reckless teen activity, it was legal for someone over eighteen to drink in bars serving lesser-potency beer in Colorado. We called them the "3.2 bars." I had barely turned eighteen when I found a circle of teens and adults older than me who frequented these places to play pool or go dancing, and I didn't need to risk getting caught with my fake ID in these bars.

I was moving around from place to place like a gypsy. I'd stay at my mother's house, Bonnie's, Lorri's, and Izzy's, and work at two restaurants, so I had money for clothes, gas, and going out. I had been thinking about the next steps in my life, but more so, I was thinking about where the next drinking event would be and what I would wear.

One of these bars had a special Sunday promotion. It was a two-story bar with a male-review strip show upstairs and female mud wrestlers downstairs. Every Sunday, a few of us, often Izzy, me, and some newer and slightly older friends we'd met at some party or another, Shar and Lisa, would get dolled up to watch the male review and drink the watery beer. Later in the evening, there was an open dance floor. The female "performers" would shower, shine up, and dance with the rest of us.

I'd attended this Sunday event for a few months and had gotten to know some of these ladies. I learned that most were "entertainers" at Shotgun Willie's, a famous strip club that's endured decades in Denver. This Sunday show was a relatively lucrative and fun change of pace for them. It also allowed them to simply be patrons at the bar after the shows were over.

I really thought these ladies were something. I admired them for their looks, the sexy way they dressed, their fit bodies, and their courage as performers. There were three of them that I saw every week. When they came out on the dance floor later in the evening, I would get excited and nervous, as I knew the night would get a lot spicier. Because the beer was weak, I wasn't quite as drunk when they arrived to join the masses, so I remember the dancing. They told me what a great dancer I was and that I should work with them at Shotgun's. I felt intimidated by them and yet honored that they would want to hang out with me.

Those nights always stretched into the mornings as we often landed at a house where the "family" of an outlaw biker club lived for an after-party. I'd known many biker people from the bars where my mother had worked. I had always been drawn to them, as they were always very good to me and my mother over the years, helping with repairs around the homes we'd lived in, helping us move, being funny with their jokes, and often very loving, even if society didn't picture them that way.

They laughed loudly, spoke directly, and had a sense of intimidation just by the way they carried themselves, but the vast majority of them that I'd known were extremely protective. So, this added to the appeal of spending time with these women. They had relationships and a form of protection from the members of the club, so this was a safe place for them by the standards of safety that they held, which I truly related to.

I was honored to be welcomed in my seduced-by-criminal-power, sexual prowess, black leather, and endless-alcohol-and-drugs kind of way. I couldn't drink like many of the other people I'd partied with. I was far more of a lightweight. I could get drunk on about a six-pack of beer, but at these after-parties, we were drinking from hard liquor bottles, not cups or cans. I had always set out to stay on pace with the others but stay lucid, yet I couldn't say no to a swig from any bottle that passed my way and would be drunk faster than anyone else.

Over these few months, I also got to know these new friends a bit better. I got to know a little more about the life of an "outlaw biker," which is to say that I learned that many of them had pretty sad stories, severe drug problems, criminal backgrounds, and that while they (the men and the women) were very pretty to look at and they always had what seemed like money to blow, their lives (and souls) were as messy as mine.

Many of us had the same morning shame and hangovers. The house we'd partied at was trashed. Several mornings, I came to on the dirty floor. I'd wake up at four a.m., put on my boots, and leave to hitchhike home and get ready for work.

To speak to the caliber of some of the biker protection I referenced, I would often be walking down the block to get to the main road, and Shadow, the man who owned the home, would pull up next to me in his old custom truck and say, "Get in." He didn't like my hitchhiking in their neighborhood. "I told you to wake me."

"I never have to," I'd smile gratefully.

Shadow woke to every noise, and he'd given me rides across town numerous times that I don't think anyone knew about. We didn't talk much, but I trusted him.

I was pretty drawn to that house, those people, and the many parties we attended in places where Shadow didn't pull up like some protective father type, but I was wearing out. More lost memory. More hitchhiking home from random parts of town. Many drunken rides on a motorcycle or in a hot rod owned by the bikers, drunk, and more trips to that same bar the following Sunday... Rinse and repeat.

As I was getting sick and tired of being sick and tired, I knew I needed to make some changes. I'd been floating from drunk night to drunk night, with a few stops at my mother's for a change of clothes and an argument about how much she'd done for me.

The emotions that began to dominate all the others were anger and shame. Mix them with justification, and I felt entitled to do whatever I wanted. After all, I'd been funding my clothes, parties, and entertainment for years. I also kept telling myself that I would do better. I even believed it on rare occasions.

I'll add here that I also felt guilty for leaving my brother so often. He and I had some pretty tough times, too. I was not a great sister, daughter, or person, for that matter. He'd been old enough to stay home alone for a while, but he always wanted to spend time together, and I was just too selfish. I was too busy running away and escaping from everything that represented my childhood or home, and unfortunately, that included him.

I was manipulative, dishonest, and physically unwell, and I truly had no idea what my next move would be. I was a high school dropout, a drunk, a severe pothead, and just mystified about a great many things, especially any semblance of how to be an adult.

Shannon was going to school to become a court reporter in New Mexico. Izzy was about to graduate from high school and start cosmetology school. Bonnie had a full-time job and never really drank that much anyway, so she was a bit distant. And our new friends seemed to have it together a bit more as well. Shar had a full-time job working with her mom, and I envied how close they were. Lisa had just committed to joining a vocational training program out of state and was about to leave for Utah.

I couldn't help but compare myself. I felt like everyone that I cared about or had been spending time with had it together far better than I did, and yet, I was setting myself up to work in restaurant and bar life and nothing more.

I didn't want to be at home anymore, as it didn't feel like home. Yet, nowhere else did, either. I had dreamed of living in California and tried to imagine how to escape this life I wasn't experiencing much success in. I considered asking a few friends to get an apartment and become roommates, but I wasn't on good enough terms with anyone, as they all knew how I drank and the mess I would become almost nightly.

I knew I needed to make money, so I thought about my entertainer friends. I had gotten to know them well enough to realize that, despite some having serious drug problems, they all had money, and most had their own or shared apartments with other dancers. They had mentioned to me about coming to work with them on numerous occasions and I always said that I couldn't do what they did.

They insisted that I could; I just didn't know it yet. One of them, whom I liked more than the others, Shelly, added that she had started as a cocktail waitress, which wasn't topless, but she still made pretty good money.

So, on an impulsive whim, one sunny Thursday afternoon around one p.m. in January of 1986, I borrowed my mother's car and drove to Shotgun Willie's.

I walked in. The place was empty, and most of the lights were on. I'd been in there maybe two other times before and had never seen it fully lit. The smell took me straight back to memories of the Oak Alley Inn, a dive bar my mother worked at when I was small.

In times when my stepfather was out at some bar and didn't get home in time for our mom to leave for work, her only option for a babysitter on short notice was the shack with a mattress on the floor behind the Oak Alley Inn. I hated that shack. It was scary, dirty, smelly, and there was never any sleeping with the loud bar twenty feet away. The smell of spilled beer, other booze, and cigarettes was strong.

The memory of that shack was like a PTSD episode. The smell, the smoke, the boisterous, loud talking, and laughter came to mind as I considered what Shotgun's was like on a busy night.

I shook off the memory of the shack and thought about the money I could make, getting my own place, and the idea of being as sexy as I'd thought my dancer friends were, but not having to be topless felt like a solution.

I looked around to see if I could find someone to ask about a job. The only person I saw was the bartender. He was behind the bar, taking bottles out of boxes, so I walked down to that end of the bar and stood there until he noticed me.

"I heard you might be hiring for cocktail servers," I said when he looked up.

He didn't say anything in reply. He just handed me a paper application and a pen and walked away. I literally heard his thought as he gave me the paper and looked me up and down: *You'll be stripping in no time.*

I walked to the other end of the bar because I felt a little creeped out by the way he looked at me. I sat on the stool closest to the door and looked around the bar. I looked at the stages and the dancing poles on each one. I envisioned the place packed and truly considered if I could dress sexy and allow the men to gawk at me and make passes as they watched the strippers and I handed them drinks. I tried to envision myself dancing topless in front of drunk strangers, taking heed of the bartender's thoughts and my conversation with Shelly, knowing she started as a cocktail server but became a stripper.

I began to feel a little queasy.

Again, I shook it off and thought about the money and having my own apartment; I then looked at the application. I had barely finished writing my first name when a strong feeling that something was wrong with this picture came over me. I thought about the track marks on the one girl's arm. I thought about how they'd talked to each other at some of the after-parties on those Sunday nights. They were not *really* friends with each other. They were competitors for stage tips and who could dress more provocatively. I thought about selling out beyond the job of cocktail waitress and how the idea of breaking the chain was slipping further and further away.

Do I really want this?

As I went to write my last name, I got emotional. I wasn't sure what name to write. I knew I'd need a fake ID, as I'd lost my last one. I wasn't sure if I could request a specific name on a new fake ID, but I knew that my legal last name was not my actual name. It was the last name of the man listed on my birth certificate, and suddenly I was lost.

I had no idea who I was. I had no connection to my paternal bloodline, no connection to my future, the connections to those I cared about were weak, and there I was considering becoming an "entertainer."

I was aware that the money would be dirty, the life I knew these ladies were living was dirty, and the chain that I wanted to break would wrap around my soul like that tight ankle strap of those seven-inch heels they wore.

Many of them had just as much damage from their childhood as I did, and while they were all just getting by, like anyone else, the ones I'd gotten to know weren't living a life that had anything to do with breaking these chains I'd been so convinced I'd somehow break.

And clear as the sky is blue, I heard a voice. It was my voice. "What the fuck are you doing?" I took the application with me as I walked out. I ripped it into several pieces, threw it in the garbage can outside the main entrance, got in my mother's car, and drove away.

This particular memory is one of the first good decisions I ever made on instinct. I had had several close calls with death, the law, and injury over those last several years of my insanity, so much so that I had always known that I was protected in some way.

However, this choice was an act of clearly knowing that I needed to walk away, and I walked away quickly without ever looking back. It was my first moment of true clarity, and it altered my life forever.

CHAPTER 9

The Beginning of the End

"MOST OF THE SHADOWS OF THIS LIFE ARE CAUSED BY STANDING IN ONE'S OWN SUNSHINE."
~ RALPH WALDO EMERSON

AS I WALKED OUT OF SHOTGUN WILLIE'S and got in the car to drive back to my mother's house, I was overwhelmed by the awareness that I needed a change. This long-held ideal of breaking free from the chains of my family patterns was quite evident in that moment. It was time to move on with my life. And I believe I had my second moment of clarity, just moments after the first.

I thought of Lisa and her too-good-to-be-true plan.

Lisa and I met on September 16, 1985, at a 3.2 bar. We were dancing, and friends were cheering with the watered-down beer, yelling, "Happy Birthday!" It was my eighteenth birthday and her nineteenth. When we realized it was the same day, our friendship began. She became one of the friends I spent a lot of time with in those months leading up to my moment of clarity at Shotgun Willie's.

I'd only known her for a few months when she told me about the Job Corps of America program in Utah and how she'd earn her GED and learn a trade. She said that she was going to learn how to paint cars. She was a very talented artist who could scribble a masterpiece on a cocktail napkin in seconds. Painting cars and adding custom art designs to them was a vision she shared, which was easy to support.

She saw that this was an opportunity, and couldn't wait to get out of Colorado, as she had been partying pretty hard and wasn't getting along too well with ideas of her adult future either. She had heard me talk about my dream of moving to California often, so she tried to talk me into going with her to Job Corps, and then moving to California together, but it had seemed too good to be true, so I had dismissed it.

In that moment, I remembered her saying she had to meet with a guy downtown for her plane ticket a week or so prior, so I drove to the nearest payphone, opened the big heavy phone book, and looked up the address for the Job Corps office. I didn't call. I just drove straight downtown to their office, parked (probably illegally), and walked in.

I was wearing a pair of shiny black spandex pants, a strategically cut-up T-shirt with the name of the band *Yes* on it, and no bra. Completely appropriate to apply for a job at a strip club, but not so much for an office building in downtown Denver.

Just walking into the building and getting on the elevator, the people in business clothing, wearing suits, dresses, and shiny pumps, were all glaring at me. I looked like the stripper I almost became as I got on the elevator to the twelfth floor.

I walked into the office and saw a sea of cubicles and fluorescent lights, then walked up to the front reception desk. No one was sitting in the chair behind the desk, so I grabbed one of the brochures and opened it when a Hispanic man in brown slacks, a white shirt, and a tie approached and asked, "Can I help you?"

"A friend of mine just left for Utah, and I just came to ask more about what the program is," I said, but then felt immediately nervous as I was dressed so inappropriately to be asking for such an opportunity that would include them paying for me to fly to Utah.

I wish I could remember his name, because he made me feel so important in that moment. I would thank him if I could.

"Do you have some time to fill out the application?" He asked with a smile.

"I do," I replied.

"Follow me," he said as he walked back to his cube by a window overlooking the Denver skyline.

He had two chairs on the other side of his desk. He opened a drawer, took out a document, and clipped it to a clipboard. It was four pages inside and out, and I filled out every detail.

I didn't think twice about my legal surname, and I answered honestly about only finishing tenth grade. There were several multiple-choice questions that I know today were more personality test-related, such as, "Do you tend to speak more openly, or are you shy?" with four or five options ranging from strongly agree to strongly disagree. Several others were more logistical about age, race, gender, etc.

He had stepped away while I completed it, and when I finished, I stood up to look out the window. I imagined what it would be like to have a job in an office in one of these buildings. I imagined what kind of professional style I would have based on the people I'd seen in the building's lobby. I felt uncomfortable again, knowing I was in a professional office without a bra on. My mother would have been appalled.

When he came back and we sat down at his desk, he reviewed the application and confirmed a few things I'd written, then explained that the United States Department of Labor funded this program for youth between the ages of sixteen and twenty-four. He told me I could go voluntarily, but that many students under eighteen had been sent there as an alternative to juvenile hall. He said it was a last chance for many young people, but then he told me why someone like me was a perfect candidate, as if he didn't care at all about how inappropriately I was dressed.

He shared that the students who joined voluntarily had a high success rate in education, job placement, and longer-term life achievements. He told me about the numerous centers across the United States and the many trades I could consider. He explained that the program included a paycheck every two weeks and housing, clothing, and food. One of the benefits that impressed me the most was a monthly deposit into a "readjustment fund" for when I left the program. He told me that I could get my GED as well as a high school diploma and described their vocational training for office jobs, since I told him that was my interest.

About ninety minutes after I had entered that office, he gave me a few papers, including a plane ticket, instructions on what to pack and what not to pack, and a handshake. I was heading to the Clearfield Job Corps center in Clearfield, Utah. It had the best office skills vocational training and was the second largest Job Corps center in the US, with over 1,500 students.

I left that building with a sense of fear and worry that I wouldn't be able to do well in any kind of program like this, a newfound hope because I was given the opportunity to try anyway, and a sense of relief that I'd be leaving Colorado.

When I returned to my mom's place, my mom and brother were in the kitchen together. He was eating at the table, and she was getting a soda from the refrigerator.

"I'm moving to Utah." I held up my plane ticket.

My brother grabbed the ticket to look at it and said, "Why?" He was stunned, and I could see that he was upset.

"Don't you think you should have asked?" My mother was offended that I'd made such a life decision, such as this, without considering talking to her.

"About what? How to get my life together? From you? I'm eighteen, I don't need to ask."

She shook her head and held her hand out to see the papers I had in my hand. As she started to look at them, I glanced at my brother and realized I had just been too harsh.

I apologized for my harsh retort and told my mom and brother about the program. When my mom heard that Lisa was already there, she felt better about my going.

We may not have gotten along well, but I knew that any friend of mine was a friend of hers and she'd met Lisa. One of my mother's good traits was her acceptance of my friends. So, I knew this was important to share.

I was talking to them both, but mostly looking at my brother.

I felt his sadness that I was leaving, so I just kept talking about the program, hoping he'd soften and be happy for me.

"When do you go?" my brother asked.

"I leave in three weeks."

My brother had been listening to me rattle, and I could feel him getting sad and angry. I'd already spent so much time away that I felt he was getting used to it, but in this moment, I also realized he missed me, and now I would not just be gone a lot, but I was moving away, far away.

I walked over to him and put my arm around his shoulder and said, "I'm going to miss you so much."

"Yeah, right."

"I am." I realized that I truly would. "Let's do something special before I go," I said, not knowing if I'd honor it, just feeling like it may make up for all of my absence and insensitivity to his life and likely his own loneliness and disconnect. We may not have gotten along great or even spent much time together, but we were close as siblings and loved each other, so I did feel true guilt for leaving him.

The guilt and compassion for him weighed on me, but not as much as the desire to get away from my life and all of the temptation and self-destruction.

I had legal trouble, too.

In the first eighteen months of having a driver's license, I had received several traffic tickets for everything from speeding to running red lights (yet hadn't been caught drunk driving). I had so many that my license was suspended. I had a court date that was after my departure to Utah, but it didn't seem nearly as relevant as getting out of dodge.

So, off I went to Job Corps.

It's funny to me that some things are so clear and some are so foggy, but I remember arriving on a Tuesday in February of 1986. It was a sunny day in Utah, and it was warm. A van driver with a Job Corps red windbreaker held a sign that had my name on it. As he drove me and six others to campus, I admired the Utah landscape. While they weren't the Rocky Mountains I was used to, there were some beautiful mountain views, and the clouds reminded me of the skies in Colorado, which are often blue with a skyscape that makes looking up a natural instinct.

When we drove through the entry gates, I was surprised by the vastness of it. The center was situated on eighty-four acres of land, with brick buildings as far as the eye could see, a variety of trees of different species and sizes, and lush, green grass.

The first stop was a building right by the main gate for registration and dorm assignment. Then, a ride in a golf cart to my dorm so I could unpack.

As instructed, I went back outside to wait for the golf cart to pick me up for the bigger tour of the center. I tuned out a bit as we rode around, and I took in the idea that this was my new residence. I caught where the pool, theater, classes, and cafeteria were, and I could tell the student giving the tour enjoyed the job. I even considered what I'd look like in one of the red windbreakers.

After the tour, it was already time for dinner, so I met up with Lisa and we had dinner together and she took me to her dorm to show me where she stayed. She was in the dorm right next to mine, and I was relieved. Moving to another state on my own was the boldest action I'd ever taken in my young life. It was a relief to know that I had a friend there.

I didn't sleep well the first night. I heard every noise in the dorm. I tossed and turned in my tiny twin bunk. I could hear some girls in the dorm down the hall talking, and those in my room, I heard breathing as they slept.

The next morning, I got ready, met Lisa for breakfast, and went to the building to take the GED test. I was pretty intimidated by the idea of taking the test, and it must have shown on my face because the instructor quickly explained that it was given as early as possible so that they could assess what I needed to pass it.

So, I sat down, and she handed me the booklet and a pencil.

There were five sections, each timed. I completed the last section and handed the booklet to the instructor. She looked surprised when I turned it in.

Her look made me nervous. I was sure I had blown it but was relieved it was done for that day. I could study and pass it soon enough.

When I came in the next day, she said, "Congratulations, you passed." Then she added excitedly, "And you have a very high score!"

We sat down to discuss it, and she explained that I'd completed the test very quickly (which explained her look of surprise). She also said that my score might afford me some college-level classes at the center if that was of interest to me.

I listened to her but had difficulty understanding what she was saying. I was shocked. My first thought was that she might be cutting me a break for some reason. I had a tough time realizing that I'd actually passed on my first try. I knew that academics came naturally to me, but with the volume of missed classes and the deep feeling of failure for dropping out, I was in disbelief.

And then I had a moment in my thoughts: *Maybe I'm actually smart.*

I had no significant achievements before this, so I wasn't sure what to do with myself. I'd been able to earn some money, I never missed work even when I was deathly hungover, and I did pass all of my classes while in high school despite poor attendance and overly busy transcripts. But this... This was a formally documented achievement. I was not only proud of myself but a little blown away at this new taste of what success felt like. It was an unfamiliar feeling, and all I knew was that I wanted more.

When I decided to join the program, I'd also made an internal decision to get a grip on my use and abuse of substances. I had had many internal and even soulful moments in which I would admit alcoholism or addiction to myself.

There I was, with an opportunity to do something with my life to change the trajectory, and during the week, I took that very seriously. I showed up on time, dressed well, and participated. I accepted a role with the orientation committee and was proud of my red windbreaker. I also got a job managing the movie theater at the center for a little extra money. I had been one of only two students, chosen out of 1,500, to represent the center across the country in a panel discussion about the program's value. All of this landed me a photo on the cover of the orientation brochure and a couple of trips to speak about the program.

I felt really good about my achievements. None of them seemed to be overly difficult and I moved through the phases very quickly. I saw a side of myself that made it clear to me that a very different life from the one I had imagined was a true possibility.

However, there were many opportunities to drink and obtain drugs, too—many of which I took, regardless of my gaining awareness that I had some potential in life. I smoked pot daily under the justification that I was very minimally altered, and I believed that it helped me think. They had no reason to drug-test me based on my overall performance, so I got away with this easily and, in my mind, felt very little guilt about being altered by the use of marijuana.

However...

Weekends came every week. There was a Friday and Saturday bus ride to either Salt Lake City or Ogden, Utah, for entertainment or errands such as shopping for trade-related clothing (which they provided funds for) or personal items unavailable on campus. I took that bus to town with several other students every weekend.

Being among fellow troublemakers, no matter our reason for participating in the program, made it easy to leave my good intentions at the center when we left. We would get off the bus and promptly find our preferred vices. Getting alcohol and drugs in the city was even easier than when at the center, so regardless of my accolades and success while on campus, with every weekend came the all-too-familiar, drunken escapades, hangovers, and guilt.

I honestly don't know how I got away with it. I don't know how I made it back to the bus when it was time to return to the center. I just woke up in my dorm the next morning.

The weekends reminded me of the shame of having alcoholism and the way I behaved at home. Yet, I'd completely swept the shame under a rug as soon as I got to class on time Monday morning. It was like changing the station on the radio. I'd tune into the party or the class, whichever I needed to, and the bigger picture of any risk I was taking was not a consideration.

There were also a few trips home. I went home for my nineteenth birthday in September of 1986, the holidays, and the trip for my mother's fourth wedding in May of 1987. Each of these trips came with the familiar recklessness. I'd get home, call up the same old party buddies, and spend most of my time in town drunk.

The difference was that many of the friends I'd partied with before I left, like Shar, Izzy, the entertainers, and even the biker folk, weren't all that happy to see me. I'd basically disappeared without telling anyone I was going, then reappeared as if nothing had changed.

But a great deal was changing...

Not only was I discovering this part of myself that had a desire to be successful, but I was also realizing I had genuine capability when I applied myself. It made for a deep inner conflict. I had a taste of my potential over this first year in the program. As I neared the completion of the program, I also matured a bit. There was a lot of inner reflection between drinking less because it was only on the weekend and having to decide what I would do when I graduated from the program. It was the beginning of a connection to some self-awareness that I feel many young people gain in their mid-teens, but I was approaching twenty.

During our time at Job Corps, Lisa met a really cool guy named Billy, and they dated for a few months. They were the two people I spent the most time with. She and Billy had seen me drunk and volatile, and they'd seen me dressed up in my office best and speaking at a graduation or orientation event. They were the ones who told me what I did the next day. They were the ones who laughed at me and with me. They heard my weekend confessions about how I knew I was an alcoholic, and in the same sentence, about how I wanted to break the family chain and live a successful life with a career and family.

My friendship with them and my talks with them were the compass that was guiding me to more clarity that my only solution was to stop drinking.

We often spent time in the park area of the center, lying in the grass or sitting at a picnic table, having these deep, meaningful talks about our lives and hopes for our future. Billy was going to go into construction, and Lisa was going to be an artist with every medium she could get her hands on. We had this beautiful comfort with one another, and it was a safe and sacred space to just lie under the sky and offer each other an ear, our honest opinions, and the best encouragement we knew how to offer for our age and station in life. It was a glimpse of connection to authenticity, vulnerability, and trust in friendships in adulthood.

A bittersweet moment from one of those nights lying under the stars was when we'd been talking as we always did, and a humiliating memory of one of our nights in town came to mind.

I was wasted that night and started yelling at Billy for God knows what, and I tried to put him in a headlock with the intention of physically fighting. I don't remember much else about the night, or why I was yelling, except that he pushed me away from him and I stumbled backward onto someone's very wet front lawn, soaking my jeans. As I sat on the ground, a bit stunned, he yelled back at me to knock it off and that I was too drunk. I thought highly of Billy, so of all the nights to remember, this one was very humiliating.

They'd been talking for a bit, and I was quiet in my reflection and embarrassment.

"Hey, you still with us?" Lisa asked, noticing my silence and sensing my contemplation.

"I really shouldn't drink anymore," I said, and my eyes welled up with tears. "It's really hard to think that I'm actually an alcoholic."

"You're pretty tough, though," Billy said. "You could stop."

Lisa just reached over and took my hand.

It was a profound yet brief moment of knowing what I *needed* to do, yet having no idea how to do it, or if I even really believed my own words. Even more profound was that neither of them offered a shred of protest.

Over the next three months, I achieved an honor-four status, which was the highest level of student status one could obtain. I had completed my GED, finished my vocational training, and then received my high school diploma as well. I was what they called a Complete Program Graduate.

At the program completion graduation ceremony, I was the main speaker. My mom even made the trip to Utah for my graduation with a good friend of the family. I was truly happy to see her, too. She was beaming with pride for and with me.

I had a great deal to be proud of in terms of my accomplishments and prestige within the program. Yet, there was an equal amount of shame about my drinking exploits and the heritage I blamed for them. This entire experience, despite its bittersweet taste, was incredibly valuable. I had connected with a part of myself I hadn't met before, the part that was intelligent, capable, and humbly beginning to awaken. This was the beginning of the end of the disconnect.

CHAPTER 10

Hitchhiking in Sacramento

"ONE MOMENT CAN CHANGE A DAY. ONE DAY CAN CHANGE A LIFE
AND ONE LIFE CAN CHANGE THE WORLD."
~ BUDDHA

WHEN I COMPLETED JOB CORPS and returned to Colorado in mid-August of 1987, I stayed with my mother, stepdad, and brother. I had to wait three weeks to get my readjustment check for $1,800 for completing the program. While I was there, I was really starting to feel conflicted about my next steps.

I had sincere trepidation about staying in Colorado because by then, I had matured enough to realize I simply couldn't trust myself. Within the first week of being home, I was out every night that my mom worked and would let me have the car. I drove to the biker house and did the same old dance that I'd done every time I'd been there before; drink, ride on the motorcycles at night, get in the hot rods to cruise with drunk drivers, but there was also a knowing that it wasn't the same. It was a knowing that it would never be the same again.

I would never be the same again.

I'd been absent for eighteen months, and I had some semblance of direction. I had previously loved this aimless circle of partiers who were content in the daily grind of work, spending all of their money on the party, waking up ashamed and aimless, and doing it all over the next day to bury the shame and disconnect. No judgment of one another, just recycling the aimlessness.

I was intentionally attempting to drink less, but each time I told myself that I would only drink a few, the alcohol hit my system, and I would lose my sense of judgment about how much I drank. I will say that because I did attempt to control it, I did remember more. The lost memory was still happening, just not as early in the evenings. I remember feeling out of place and uncomfortable, as I simply wasn't as welcome. And while I didn't quite know it yet, I didn't want to be in this scene anymore either.

Somewhere in that first week back home, I called Bonnie to catch up. She had moved to California with her mother, and I mentioned how awesome I thought it was that she lived there now.

"You could move here with us if you wanted to, you know," she said casually.

She'd heard me talk about moving to California for a few years, and her family had always welcomed me into their home. So, this was a dream offer.

"Really?" I replied. "Do you think your mom would be okay with that?"

"Of course. We don't have to live with her forever. We could get our own place too."

I was excited, and the plan was in motion. Get the check, buy a trailer, haul ass to California and live the dream.

I spent the next couple of weeks planning, discussing the plan incessantly, and packing. In my intention to drink less, I spent some time with my grandmother talking about the number of letters we'd sent back and forth while I was in Utah. She was the only one I wrote to while I was away, and I cherished her letters. I made a concerted effort to reconnect with her, not knowing when I'd be home again.

I gave Jeff a few of my albums and some other things he wanted and went to see Lorri, too. I also stopped by all the family hangouts to say my goodbyes and have a few illegal bar drinks with them.

When I got my check, I bought the back end of an old pickup truck that had a trailer hitch. Bonnie's brother Joe and his friend Greg said they would hook it up to Greg's car and drive me out there. This way, Joe could see his mom and Bonnie too.

Lisa's dad also lived near Sacramento, so when I told Lisa, she asked if she could catch a ride with us to go stay with her father and see about finding a job in auto-body there. She had been working for a house-painting company in Denver and hated it.

I loved that someone I trusted would drive us there, and I was excited that I would be living in California with both Lisa and Bonnie. The plan felt perfect!

When we mapped out our route to Sacramento, we decided to leave on September 13th, so that we could arrive in Sacramento before Lisa and my birthday on September 16th and celebrate with Bonnie. We also decided to take a longer route so we could stop in Los Angeles and see the ocean. Neither Joe, Greg, nor I had ever seen the ocean, so this was another exciting prospect.

Over the next few days of getting packed and mapping our trip, I made a commitment to myself that I wasn't going to smoke any cigarettes, any pot, drink anymore, or get myself in any bad situations from the moment we hit the road. I truly believed that this was going to be a magical, life-changing road trip that would lead to my new and successful life.

But alas...

Joe and Greg liked to drink as much as I did. Add in the delusion that a road trip is a big party, and we should be drinking and celebrating our open road freedom, well, I didn't make it an hour out of Denver before the justifications set in.

This is probably my last big hoorah, was the gist of my thinking. I broke every promise to myself before I made it to the state line. I was smoking cigarettes and pot and drinking with the boys. Lisa drank some, but never as much as I did.

Joe and I had started arguing over some drunken event from several years prior. We were like family, as I'd also spent a lot of time at his and Bonnie's house as a teen. He was still angry at me for stealing and losing a pendant from his room. I didn't remember taking it, and certainly didn't remember losing it, but it was very sentimental to him. I had apologized for this numerous times over the years, but mixing alcohol and unresolved offenses in a car on a road trip makes for a sour cocktail.

What should have taken us less than two days took us four and a half days. Greg and Joe were our drivers, and they were supposed to be rotating shifts. However, they were often too drunk to drive, so we spent several hours passed out at rest stops and on the shoulders of the road.

When we finally made it to Los Angeles on the third day, it was late morning. We pulled into Santa Monica. Joe initially chose to stay in the car, and Lisa and Greg went immediately to the shoreline of the ocean. I walked to the beach and sat in the sand. It was another of those deeply bittersweet moments.

I had a fleeting sense of what a cool birthday present it was as I sat by the ocean in California, on my twentieth birthday. And what I had imagined would be a great moment was crushed by shame and deep humiliation that I couldn't even make it an hour out of Denver before I blew it. I hadn't only drunk, but Joe and I had also ruined the whole trip for each other and our friends.

After a while, Joe finally got out of the car and came and sat down next to me.

"Happy Birthday," he said with his head hanging down, as he felt the shame of it all, too.

"Thank you," I said, but couldn't quite take my eyes off the ocean.

"Truce?" he asked.

"Please," I replied, adding, "I love you like family. I really am sorry." I paused for a minute, then added, "Can we please not drink for the rest of the trip?"

"I'm not the one with the drinking problem," was his response. And while we both had a drinking problem, I simply got quiet. I wasn't considering his problem. I was ashamed of mine. Make no mistake, his words hurt my feelings, but I was tired of fighting. I just wanted to take in this moment.

We stood up and walked to the water with Lisa and Greg, and she yelled, "I'm twenty-one!"

We were in Los Angeles on a beach, and it was Lisa's twenty-first birthday. If there was ever an excuse to blow off your sober intentions again, even two minutes later, well, I'm betting you can guess how the rest of that stop went. We didn't leave L.A. until the next morning, day four.

However, we did stay sober for the seven hours it took us to get to Sacramento.

It was really good to see Bonnie and to finally arrive. She gave us a hard time for how long we took to get there, but the next few days were actually quite nice.

We dropped Lisa at her dad's a few hours after unloading my things from the trailer and we all enjoyed the time together with Joe and Bonnie's mom before Greg and Joe headed back.

Now, I'll start my life, I thought.

However, things started off a bit rocky. Without experience, I struggled to get an office job, and the Sacramento public transportation system was far more difficult to navigate than Denver's. So, I impulsively bought a cheap 1978 Chevrolet Chevette from a local dealership with the last bit of my Job Corps money. Having a car seemed like the solution, but it was quite a beater. It had a broken radiator, a cracked windshield, a radio that didn't work, and a stick shift that I didn't know how to drive. So, I gratefully took advantage of California's Lemon Law to return it two days later.

So, there I was, feeling a bit defeated as my big solution didn't work out. I was a young adult, an immature alcoholic with $200 in my pocket and my thumb out on the strip in Sacramento.

An old, faded yellow Audi with loud music pulled over, and the driver rolled down his passenger window. "Are you working, or do you just need a ride?" said the long-haired, tattooed guy with the leather vest. His appearance reminded me of Shadow.

I had no idea what he meant, as I didn't know Sacramento well enough to know I was on the strip. So, I thought I was being witty when I replied, "How about I just need a ride to work?" and got in the car.

"I'm JC."

"Thanks for the ride, JC. I'm Paula."

I told him where I needed to go, and we started chatting. I told him about my car-buying adventure/fail and how I was new to Sacramento. Based on his long hair, tattoos, and the rock and roll music he played on the radio, I assumed that he was the drinking and drugging type, so I told him I had a little money if he wanted to party.

"I don't drink or use drugs."

Now, in my limited time on earth in 1987, I didn't know any long-haired, tattooed, rock and roller type who didn't drink or use drugs, so I got scared. I thought to myself, *Well, this is it. Your luck has run out, and you finally got in the wrong car.*

I tensed up and got quiet.

I think he sensed how quickly my energy changed because he went on to say, "I've been clean for a year now. I'm in Narcotics Anonymous."

I knew what that meant. Shannon had told me about the nice people from Narcotics Anonymous, so my fear immediately settled and turned to curiosity.

"So, how do you do it?"

He told me about how he and his friends went on motorcycle rides and campouts, how many of them went to these big dances, and had these great rides down the river on rafts, all without the use of drugs and alcohol. I knew about meetings from Shannon, but I didn't know about this side of the twelve-step programs, so I was fascinated.

I remember thinking how badly I needed to be around people who didn't drink or use drugs, so when he dropped me off, we exchanged numbers and agreed to stay in touch.

For weeks, we called each other with different intentions. I would ask him about weekend events, like a dance or a motorcycle ride, but his car would be broken down. He'd call when his car was running well and ask if I wanted to try one of those meetings, but I was always hesitant.

My first few months in Sacramento, I did a few temp jobs, drove cars, migrated to other drinkers, and found my way into several drunken nights and shameful mornings with difficult apologies.

"Why do you think you drink so much?" Bonnie's mom asked me one day. She never engaged with me much when I was drinking, but she tried to reach out when I was sober.

"I guess I'm an alcoholic." We had a fairly short conversation about my family and how I felt that I might grow out of it, and how conflicted I'd felt even using the word *alcoholic* at the age of only twenty.

Although, in my heart of hearts, I knew what I was. I was at a point in my drinking where there was no hiding that. I hated how much I was letting myself down and even more so that I was letting Bonnie and her mom down.

I know that when I came home drunk late at night, and woke up Bonnie and picked fights with her, that her mom would wake up too.

I'd go for a few days without drinking at all and just smoking pot. Then, on day four or five, I'd drink to excess, create drama, wake up sick, hungover, embarrassed as hell, and apologize.

I was as sick of it as they were and just so confused about how this kept happening.

Yes, a part of me was very clear about how it kept happening. I took the first drink. That led to a thousand more. That led to any other substances that were available, like cocaine, mushrooms, acid, and then, of course, more alcohol.

Bonnie and I did finally move out of her mom's place into a furnished two-bedroom apartment. Without parental authority, I drank more, and we argued more.

Bonnie was the most unconditionally loving friend I'd had in my life. She loved the sober side of me and saw beyond my drinking to the version of me that I wanted to be. But now that we were "adults" living without any limits of what a parent may think, we were beginning to grow apart.

The disconnect was just as present as it had been most of my life. I was disconnecting from hope, from Bonnie, and was in the beginning of disconnecting from the idea that I could ever change because I was destroying my California dream.

One Monday night, I decided to go to my coworker's band's show in a storage garage. I asked Bonnie to come, but she said no. She'd been declining every effort I'd made to go out together for a while, but I kept asking because I always felt safer with her, and I wanted to keep trying to not only heal our fighting but also this alcohol induced amnesia thing.

As my denial got deeper, I began to think that I would stop blacking out if I just kept trying. It was such a delusional thought after blacking out for eight years nearly every time I drank, but somewhere in the denial, I made up this thought that I would outgrow it.

I set out with the intention that I would just have a few that night. However, I awoke to one of the guys in the band shaking my shoulder. I had passed out on one of the sofas and it was after midnight. I remember batting his hand away at first and then realizing it was my friend.

I don't remember walking home. I vaguely remember fighting with Bonnie and standing at the refrigerator with the door open. I remember the look of disgust on Bonnie's face and that we had both been very loud and very angry. One thing I did remember was Bonnie forcefully yell-whispering, "Keep it down! The neighbors can hear you!"

Later, I woke up and looked over at my clock. It was 6:30 a.m. I was late for work. I tried to sit up so I could go call my boss, and my head hurt so bad that I just laid back down. If I'm honest, I was still a bit drunk. I *had* to make this call, so I did make myself get up a few minutes later. I felt a little weak in my legs when I stood up, and all I wanted to do was lie back down.

I made it to the phone and called my boss at the diner and told them I was sorry, but that I had the flu.

I'd never missed work before, even the six a.m. shifts. So, this was a new low. I missed work because of my drinking. I was ruining my friendship with Bonnie because of my drinking. I was physically immobilized because of my drinking. I was an asshole because of my drinking, and the shame that overcame me that morning was deep and incomprehensible. I sincerely contemplated if drinking was going to be what killed me before I even turned twenty-one.

As I lay back down and the shame deepened, I had a flashback to the night that I did die.

I'd minimized this event so many times, but I knew what it was. I was seventeen, and it was a snowy night in Denver when some friends were out picking up one another in a big 4 x 4 truck, so we could all go get snowed in and party at a house we frequented. I'd been sick with a bad cold, so I had taken cold medicine before they got there.

We stopped at the liquor store to stock up and proceeded to get as loaded as we could. With the combination of cold medicine, numerous shots, and too many bong hits, I must have known I was going to vomit, so I made my way to the bathroom and locked the door. The next thing I remember, I was floating above the room. I stared at my lifeless body lying in vomit on a dirty bathroom floor. I felt a warmth behind me and to my right as I slowly floated higher. I remember feeling bewildered seeing my body lying on the floor, but also feeling relief from the soft, peaceful light in my right peripheral. I don't know how long I was floating, but the contemplation felt slow.

Suddenly, on my left peripheral, there was a lot of commotion. I didn't hear anything, but I saw the doorjamb to the bathroom door splinter and break open. I saw two of my friends drop to the ground over my body to shake me and slap my face to wake me up.

I felt my soul suddenly slam back into my body, and I woke up. The denial that it was actually a near-death experience due to extreme use of alcohol and substances was strong. I'd minimized it and dismissed it numerous times, but it haunted me—especially this morning, when I missed work for the first time due to a hangover.

I was so sick. The hangovers had progressively gotten much more brutal. I could barely open my eyes, and pain and toxicity were coursing through every muscle and bone in my body. Add in the embarrassment of the band guy having to wake me up after everyone had gone, wondering if the neighbors had heard me ranting, missing work—at a diner, not an office—and the haunting memory I couldn't deny of my actual death. The mountain of shame and reality that I was dying a slow death was awful. I felt completely demoralized in that moment.

The person I'd become was not at all who I'd thought I'd be, even at the tender age of twenty. I'd grown to hate her. She was reckless, mean, and clown-like. She was becoming less and less able to manage the amount of mind-altering substances she was consuming. The bad decisions were those of someone who didn't want to live very long.

I had to reconcile that that person was me. She was in trouble, was hurting others and herself, and had lost control a long time ago.

I made my way to the bathroom and saw that I'd not fully made it to the toilet when I'd vomited the night before, which I didn't remember doing, but there was no question that it was mine.

Cleaning up vomit with a deathly hangover is an experience of both disgust and utter humility that I was all too familiar with.

I was so angry with myself and not just ashamed but bewildered. I was tired of not knowing what I was angry about those nights before. I had had so many nights of memory loss and volatility that I'd lost count by then. The unbelievable embarrassment, loss of control, and hurt feelings carried an incredible weight on my soul.

And the people I'd hurt…

I saw Shannon's face on the night of that fight in the field. I remembered so many faces laughing at me and my idiotic behavior. I remembered my brother and how I'd blown him off on many occasions when he had no one, including not doing anything special before I left. I thought of my grandmother and how I hadn't talked to her in weeks. I was too embarrassed about not doing better. There were people who cared about me, and yet there was great distance from them, one of whom I lived with.

My conscience was eating me alive.

I loved Bonnie. She'd heard my apologies for my shitty nights and the shitty fights a thousand times and continually forgave me. She saw the light in my eyes when I shared about wanting a better future. She was there for all of it, and yet, I know we both felt the strain on our friendship due to my drinking.

I don't know if I'd call it a breaking point or a moment of clarity, but I wanted it all to end. My empty promises and my weakening body so depleted me. I was sick of seeing myself in the mirror and aware that those chains I'd talked about breaking had me in a tight hold.

Something had to give.

Chapter 11

As it Turns Out...

"Even the darkest night will end, and the sun will rise."
~ Rumi

That night, when I believed I had died, kept plowing into my thoughts. It was like the railroad crossing lights flashing and warning me that if I didn't do something, I may not be alive much longer.

I thought about JC. He had called me several times to invite me to a meeting, and I'd declined and declined. Part of me felt that if I called him, he probably wouldn't take me seriously. Part of me felt I had no other option but to pick up that phone and try. It felt like my life depended on it.

"Hey, It's Paula. Are you going to one of those meetings tonight?"

He didn't flinch. "I am. If you want to go, there's a meeting at seven."

I paused for a minute. This felt scary and was so humbling. "Okay," was the best I could do.

"I'll pick you up at 6:30," and he hung up.

And now to apologize to Bonnie. Again. I'd avoided her all morning, and it was already noon. I never did go back to sleep.

I cleaned the bathroom and sat on my bed with my head in my hands, just drowning in my shame and haunting moments of recklessness. I tried to blame my mother, my stepfather, or even my sister, who had been a favorite partner in crime and also an enabler. And with every avenue I tried to place blame, the road just kept circling back to me.

It took all the humility and courage I could muster to face Bonnie, as I was as far down on myself as I had ever been.

I could hear her washing the dishes in the kitchen. I walked from my bedroom down the fifteen-foot hallway, although it felt like a mile because I was so heavy, and I sat at the table. I could feel the tension rise when I sat down.

She didn't even look at me, so I just sat there for a while until she finished.

She was drying her hands off, and I looked at her, waiting to make eye contact.

She wouldn't make eye contact and tried to walk past me, but I gently grabbed her hand, and she stopped. "I'm so sorry," I said as tears welled up. I had a few visions of our yelling from the night before, but nothing clear except the yell-whispering in my face. I just know she was completely exasperated.

"Really?" She replied. She finally looked at me with the evident frustration I felt too, but as always, she was willing to hear me out.

"Yes, truly. What I do is not okay."

"It's not. I didn't do anything to deserve that. I never do anything to deserve your bullshit."

"I know. I'm sorry. I don't drink right. I'm going to get some help."

"What does that mean?"

"I'm going to an NA meeting with that guy."

"What guy?" She asked with a sense of worry, curiosity, and a hint of an eye roll, knowing I'd hung out with a lot of random people.

"JC, the one who hasn't drank or done any drugs for over a year, who picked me up hitchhiking."

She immediately softened and sat at the table with me.

That's when the tears started to really flow. As they flowed, I told her again that I knew I had a problem, that I truly wanted to stop, and that I never wanted to hurt her or anyone else again. I don't know if she believed me, and I don't know if I believed myself, but I knew I had to try to make it right.

The majority of that day was a blur. My heart was so heavy, and I was scared and physically unwell. I had no idea what was to come, but there was this remembrance of Shannon's experience with meetings and recovery. I held the seed she had planted very close to my soul. I remembered the lightness in her voice when she talked about the people in rehab and the meetings. It was like a parachute for me that day. Somewhere in all of the aches and shaking and spiraling into shame, I had a glimmer of hope.

As it was nearing the time for my new friend to pick me up, I took a shower and got ready to go. I struggled severely with what to wear because I was nervous. I wanted to be liked by these strangers, but I was terrified of what they'd think of me. Even though I'd only met one of them, I admired and respected that they somehow had won the battle I'd been fighting for years.

I was torn between the black leather jacket and the brown leather jacket. Blue jeans or black jeans. Heels or no heels. I thought I'd be going to a room with white tile floors and fluorescent lights. I imagined ice-water pitchers and dishes with granola on the tables. I have no idea where the visual came from, and even though JC had long hair, was covered in tattoos, and wore torn and faded jeans, I just knew that most of the people there would be men in business suits or those matching sweat suits with crisp white tennis shoes.

I chose blue jeans, suede moccasins, and a white and yellow sweater. I never wore this sweater. I didn't even like yellow back then, but it had an innocence to it, so it might make a better impression. I even put a barrette on one side of my hair—again, something I *never* did.

I had thirty minutes to wait, and I was antsy. I was messing with the damn barrette in the mirror when the phone rang. It was JC, and he said that his car wouldn't start and that he was really sorry, but he couldn't make it.

Oh my God, the relief! I sat on the bed and threw the barrette across the room, and it was like the horrible morning or the even worse day of ache in my soul had never happened. The pressure I'd built up was suddenly focused on the relief of a drink. I didn't tell Bonnie, but I had a new plan! I was going to hang out with the garage band again, as if the night before had never happened.

As I picked up the phone to call the garage band friend to see if they would be playing that night, JC was on the line. I kid you not. The phone hadn't rung, but the timing was to the second. "I'm borrowing a car. I'll be there in ten!" he said in a hurry and then hung up.

There was no way I would blow him off knowing he'd borrowed a car, but man, I was torn.

All the heaviness of the day and the idea of relief with that first swig, first hit, or first second of escape from reality was enticing. Far more enticing than the barrette I picked back up and placed in my hair again...

Ten minutes passed quickly. I hugged Bonnie and was grateful I hadn't told her about the events of eleven minutes earlier. Just as he pulled up, I went outside, and we drove to the meeting.

I remember some nervous chatter, and I knew he could tell I was nervous. He tried to keep it light and make jokes, but my mind was racing. I was far too concerned about the barrette, so I took it out.

It's funny the details I remember so many years later.

The meeting was in a hall where several meetings were held daily. The meeting room was next to the gravel parking lot, and about 200 yards away was a house that looked like a little snack bar or coffee shop. Several motorcycles were lined up along the fence, and a few others were pulling in. People were milling about everywhere. The smell of exhaust was something I loved, and it was prominent.

As we walked into the meeting room, I could hear laughter and loud talking, and I saw people hugging one another. I was immediately out of place by what I'd chosen to wear, as almost everyone there wore a black leather jacket. And to my dismay, there was no ice water, granola, or even one suit of the business or jogging variety.

I had all of the pressure built up about how clean and sober people would look, and I was at the smokiest, loudest, most foul-languaged old shack in twelve-step history.

And I was in awe.

I was extremely uncomfortable, and yet, right at home. It's a feeling that only those of us who have experienced it can truly understand. They did a few introductions and asked if anyone was there for their first meeting. I looked at JC, who signaled me to raise my hand. My heart skipped a beat or two and I know my face turned red, but I raised my hand. "My name is Paula. This is my first meeting."

I was sitting right by the door, which was as comfortable as I could get. I wasn't sure if I'd ever come back as these first few minutes were as uncomfortable as I had been in years. I had no buffer of alcohol to soften the nerves, and while I'd smoked pot that day, I was still very nervous. I chain-smoked for the entire meeting, hanging on to every word each person spoke, but the only words that stuck with me were the ones they used when sharing their names.

"My name is John. I'm an addict," or "I'm an addict-alcoholic, my name is Susan."

Wow, I thought. *They said that out loud. I would never admit that to anyone.*

Part of me was appalled, and another part was in astounding admiration of their honesty. The part of me that admired their honesty realized I hadn't named my affliction when I introduced myself at the beginning of the meeting. And a whole new internal inquiry began. *Am I an addict? Or is it addict-alcoholic? God, should I even be here?*

At the end of the meeting, they called my name and asked me if I wanted to say anything. Talk about being put on the spot. The only words I could come up with were, "I'm glad to be here. The best gift anyone can give is the gift of a good example. Thank you."

I didn't say my name. I didn't admit alcoholism or addiction as I didn't know if that was my truth there, and I wanted to be honest. My honesty, in that moment, was that I just felt good being there by the end of the meeting; the rest was pure uncertainty. Then I bowed my head a little as I felt humbled by them.

Reflecting on this, I'm proud of what I said, and I'll never forget it. I felt their example more than I had any evidence of it. I felt their lightness. I felt their support for one another, and their relief at no longer living a life of active addiction or alcoholism. I felt the *connection* they shared in that walk of life.

After the meeting, several people went over to JC's place. He lived in a quadplex that faced another quadplex. They were small ranch-style units, side by side. The driveway led up in front of the four units on each side to some carports in the back, and there were cool cars. They called it Recovery Row.

I loved the vibe of this little block, if you will. They were all neighbors, and most knew each other from recovery. Many of the people I drank with, partied with, and put my life in danger with back in Colorado were so much like them, bikers, hot-rodders, and motorheads. But these people all claimed they didn't drink or use drugs. I can't say I fully trusted it, but the prospect was intriguing.

It was about nine at night, and sodas and coffee were in everyone's hands in JC's living room. I've been in a few biker-folk homes and have *never* seen a cup of coffee anywhere.

I liked coffee with cream and sugar, so I mixed it up in my Styrofoam cup and sat in a corner chair. My grandmother drank coffee all day, every day, so in a way, it felt like a comfort in a situation that was new and awkward, especially among a bunch of biker folk in that damned yellow sweater!

They were planning a motorcycle ride for Saturday together, and one of the guys who was going, Dane, didn't have a passenger, so he asked if I wanted to go along. I was honored and looked forward to the chance to redeem my choice of attire, so of course, I accepted.

JC asked Dane to give me a ride home so he would know where to pick me up on Saturday, and he agreed. On the way, he asked me what I thought about the meeting. I told him it was pretty intimidating, but I was glad I went. Then, he asked me what my drug of choice was.

I'd never been asked such a question, so it took me a minute. I'd often thought that alcohol was the most poisonous drug there was, but at the same time, I had not considered it a drug. So, I said, "I guess it's pot. I mean, I drink more than I smoke, but if we're talking drugs, it's pot."

He explained that in Narcotics Anonymous, alcohol is considered a drug, too. So, I added, "Then, it's definitely alcohol."

There was a relief in just acknowledging honestly that I had a drug of choice. Not that I'd turned down several other drugs that had been put in front of me because I hadn't. I considered my few binges on cocaine, the times I'd dropped LSD, and a few runs with meth, but as far as age and access, my go-to substance was alcohol.

The minute he dropped me off at home, I told Bonnie all about it over a few bong hits. I didn't want to use my drug of choice, as in that moment, that was pretty much all I was thinking I needed to stop if I wanted to go to another meeting or get to know these new friends.

That was a Tuesday night, and over the next four days, I did a *lot* of bong hits. I didn't touch a drop of alcohol as I didn't trust myself, and the pot helped with the shaking a little. Between the damage to my nervous system from my suicide attempt and my overuse of alcohol, the shaking was pretty bad as I was going through withdrawal.

It was weird not to drink, but I was proud of myself. I was looking forward to the Saturday ride.

JC called on Friday afternoon to tell me Dane and a few others would be there at ten a.m. on Saturday, but that he had to work. He added casually that it was probably a good idea for me not to get loaded before they arrived.

When he added that, I was a bit offended. I sincerely thought to myself, *Who gets loaded by ten a.m.? What does he think I am, some kind of alcoholic?*

I chuckle a little when I reflect on being offended by his advice.

But let me tell you that I spent the rest of that day getting as high as I could. It was as if I were trying to have some added storage for the next day. You know, like, *If this were my last day...* kind of thinking...

And as it turns out...

It was.

CHAPTER 12

One Day

"WHILE THE DARK NIGHT OF THE SOUL IS A PROCESS OF DEATH,
THE SPIRITUAL AWAKENING PROCESS IS THE REBIRTH."
~ MATEO SOL

IT WAS 10:02 AM ON SATURDAY, February 6th, 1988, when I heard the thunder of eight motorcycles rolling into my apartment complex. I felt extreme excitement and beamed with pride that an entire pack of Harleys was outside for me.

I was prepared this time. I wore black jeans, a black sweater, black leather boots, a black leather jacket, and one of my cool, black bandannas. My hair was long and curly, and I couldn't wait to feel it in the wind.

I remembered what JC had told me the day before. I hadn't smoked any pot that morning, and I hadn't had a drink since Monday.

We left Sacramento and headed toward Lake Tahoe. We stopped for lunch, and I watched as everyone ordered their drinks.

"I'll have a Coke."

"Iced tea, please."

I was genuinely surprised that not a single person ordered a drink, a beer, or a shot of any kind. I had hung out with many bikers before and was raised in the restaurant industry, so sitting around a table with fifteen biker folks and not one of them ordering an alcoholic beverage really surprised me. I knew some of them might have had alcohol as their drug of choice, but I also knew that for others it was cocaine, meth, or heroin, so I questioned why they weren't drinking if their drug of choice wasn't alcohol.

When it came time to take my order, I asked for iced tea. I'm not sure I'd ever had an iced tea over a soda before this, but many of them ordered one, so I did too.

We ate lunch, and several remarks were made about how onlookers were probably surprised that the bikers didn't have booze. I certainly was, but I kept a close eye on the behaviors of my new friends, as I just knew that eventually, there'd be a crack, and someone was going to get loaded.

I paid attention to every move they made. I kept an eye on how long they were in the bathroom, as many of the biker people I'd partied with before would be in there for a long time to get loaded on various drugs. But not one person was in the bathroom for any time beyond the necessary relief.

I paid attention to their behavior and waited for someone to become hazy-eyed, slur their words, or do anything else that might give away the secret of how they were *really* living.

They would rib each other about light-hearted things such as drinking too much coffee or belching, and I could feel how connected they were. They had many inside jokes with one another that I didn't get beyond that they were inside jokes.

We rode all over the Sacramento Valley and the Sierra Nevada area, passing through a few little towns that had been considered ghost towns but had little tourist shops. One of our stops was an ice cream parlor they'd all been to before. I remember thinking how weird it was to eat ice cream rather than drink with a bunch of bikers.

I had a very strong generalization about what I felt "these types of people" were like, and every idea I had was being shattered. I was referenced all day with statements like, "Don't scare off the newcomer," or "I bet the newcomer is surprised by our motley crew."

Let me just tell you. I was in awe.

As I write this and reflect on that day, the clearest sentiment is that I fell in love.

On the back of a motorcycle, you see beauty that the driver may miss. You get to scan the landscape and observe nature differently. And the Sierra Nevada region of Northern California is stunning.

I could truly enjoy the beauty of the snowcapped peaks in contrast with the green pine trees, the blue sky, white clouds, and black asphalt. The weather was perfect. It was probably in the mid-seventies, and the only breeze was when we flew down the road. I never got overly cold, as I had on a few rides during the winter in Colorado.

As we stopped in some small towns with old wooden buildings that were seemingly abandoned, just like you would imagine an old ghost town to look, I witnessed hugs, pats on the back, and laughter between friends who loved and trusted one another. They loved the beauty of the area too. I caught a few of them just staring off at the mountains or the beautiful cloudscapes, and it was obvious they appreciated their clear-minded views as much as I did.

I didn't like the word *newcomer*, but I felt welcomed and accepted, and they also kept an eye on me. Many times throughout the day, I was asked, "How you doin'?" from a sincere place of concern. Their intention to connect with me was sincere, and I needed it.

As the sun descended into a colorful sunset and we rode back into Sacramento in the dark, we arrived at a large warehouse to attend a speaker meeting and dance. I didn't know what to expect as I hadn't ever hung out with sober biker people. I had never been to a dance either, not even in high school, so I was open to wherever this adventure was taking me.

The parking lot was packed with at least a hundred vehicles, and there were probably two hundred or more people inside. The sheer number of people there for a twelve-step event was astonishing. It was a powerful testament to me that many people appreciated this way of life.

It had been a long day, and I was grateful despite being tired. It was an experience of the heart, and I didn't want it to end.

We all went inside, and again, there were more hugs, laughter, and ribbing of one another. Then, people were all getting settled and making their way to a spot in the sea of chairs in front of the podium. There were huge pots of coffee and a soda bar that sold candy and snacks.

I stood in the back of the room with Dane. I had a cup of coffee with cream and sugar. As it cooled that night, it was nice to feel the comfort of a warm drink and the reminder of my grandmother. I knew I had to call her and tell her about this day.

As the speaker shared her story, she said that she had been clean and sober for eight years. I literally hit Dane in the arm and exclaimed in a loud whisper, "Did you hear that!? EIGHT years?! No way!"

He looked at me a little puzzled and quickly realized I sincerely didn't believe her. He whispered back, "I know her, yes, eight years."

I remember my ears perking up, but then so did my fear. I truly wanted to stop, but for eight years?! The idea of stopping for more than just that day was daunting. I'd thought about getting loaded at least twenty times throughout the day. In fact, a large part of my time watching them all so closely that day was spent hoping for an invitation to get loaded with them, but it never came.

As the meeting ended and we were all mingling, Dane introduced me to another young woman named Jennifer. She was chatting about the speaker, and I nodded as if I related. Then she asked me a question I'd never been asked: "How long have you been clean?"

It took me aback. I had to think about what the question even meant, but in a split second, a realization hit me about the whole day and all of these people that I had newly befriended and immediately admired.

It's a split second I'll remember clear as day for the rest of my life. The thought that hit me by surprise was, *They collect time.*

It was a sudden, wild realization that sank like an anchor in a deep ocean. I understood with a deep clarity that they truly didn't use any mind-altering substances, no matter what their drug of choice was. I realized that the reason they were so sharp, grounded, funny, clearheaded, and connected for the entire day was because there were *no* drugs in use. The deeper realization was that they collect the days, weeks, months, and years since the last time they'd abused a substance, and I was more awake in that moment than I had ever been in my life.

Then, I answered her, "One day."

Over the last eight years of my young life up to that point, I sincerely don't think I'd had even one day clean *and* sober. I had had some substance in my bloodstream that would alter my emotions or mindset almost every day since the first time I got drunk at twelve.

The rest of that conversation is a blur. I remember her mixed expressions of hope and doubt that I'd make it to day two.

As the night went on, the dance was in full swing. I watched intently as they danced and laughed, and the music took over the evening. Many were great dancers, and I was in awe of how comfortable they were without drugs and alcohol. I was even invited to dance, and I did!

Day one, clean and sober, is a day I'll never forget. I met and connected with kindred spirits who truly befriended me. I witnessed light in the eyes of those who proclaimed to be drug addicts and alcoholics. I smiled from a place I had no idea was even within me. And I fell in love. I fell in love with being clean and sober and wanting nothing more than a million more days just like this.

PART II

Connection

CHAPTER 13

Three Days

"INTEGRITY IS DOING THE RIGHT THINK WHEN NO ONE IS WATCHING."
~ C.S. LEWIS

IT WAS A TUESDAY. I WOKE UP feeling contemplative. I'd been to seven meetings in three days. I hung on every word the people spoke in those meetings, but if you asked me what they said, I don't remember; it's all a haze. I just knew that the resonance was like feeling right at home, like I belonged. I didn't know them well, but there was relatability and a connection to so many of them. More so, there was the comfort of just being in the rooms with them. They spoke a language that I understood, a language of shame, soul wounds, bad choices, lack of control, and most of all, a desire to do better, be better, and recover from all of it.

I remember feeling as though I needed to be there. It was a place where I couldn't get me, where my alcoholism couldn't get me. I remember it feeling like my life depended on it.

And it did.

As I lay in bed that morning with my newfound comfort in the smell, taste, and temperature of a fresh cup of hot coffee, I processed my thoughts about the last three days. I looked around my bedroom as I slowly sipped my coffee and noticed the texture of the walls more. The paint was a pale mint green, and I could see where a previous tenant had hung a piece of art. The dirt that surrounded the frame that was no longer there was faint, but I saw it that morning. I had never noticed it before. I had a drawing of a horse that Lisa had done on a handkerchief taped to the wall, too. I didn't want to put thumbtacks in it, so I put rounded circles of tape behind each corner to stick it to the wall, because it had never occurred to me to get it framed. I marveled at it like I had seen it for the first time. The black pencil art was so precisely drawn on a thin cotton cloth. It was remarkable and perfect, frame or no frame. I had an overwhelming feeling of gratitude for my clarity. I was awake in a way that felt new, as if my senses were heightened. Truth be told, I'm sure they were.

I didn't have to be at work until four p.m. and planned to go to a meeting at noon, but I had this morning to sleep in. Yet, I couldn't sleep. I was just stirring in the wonder of it all when something profound hit me like a ten-foot wave.

I'd been clean and sober for three days.

I remembered where I was, who I was with, and what I had done the nights before, three days in a row. I hadn't raged at anyone, lied, or tried to manipulate anyone for three whole days.

This feeling of not having to feel ashamed or embarrassed or make up some lie about something I dropped the ball on was an incredible relief. It was one of the most significant moments of my early recovery and, dare I say, one of the most pivotal epiphanies of my life. For three whole days, my conscience was clean.

I had always been conscious of the majority of my poor choices of words, actions, or deeds. Whether sober or upon reflection of the out-of-control drunken behavior that I was haunted by, I was aware that there were poor choices. However, until this point, I hadn't changed my behavior. I continued to walk a life of compulsive and impulsive reactions, and there I was, not impulsively, but instinctively, making good choices. The reflection of this stark contrast was vividly apparent.

I reflected on the events of the day, just one week earlier, when I attended my first meeting. I was awake that morning, too. I was ready to change my behavior, stop drinking, and was deeply apologetic for my ways. I found the courage to call JC and ask him to take me to a meeting. Yet, the second he initially said that he couldn't come, the choice to face my drinking went out the window, and the impulse to blow off my sweet and sincere apology to Bonnie was thrown away just as quickly as the barrette in my hair. The contrast of my willingness to change, face the music, and get it together, with the memory of how that swift impulsiveness to simply blow all of that off stung as much as the revelation that it didn't go that way felt like music to my spirit.

I had a keen awareness of right and wrong. I didn't make one bad choice for which I didn't feel a sense of guilt and shame. However, I hadn't been astute enough to identify or name these emotions with any specificity, much less choose how to handle them with any level of maturity or awareness of how to make them right. I just knew that if I didn't like how I felt, I would attempt to escape it. The choices were never healthy ways to address emotional expression, just temporary fixes to avoid feeling anything negative.

The pattern of escapism seemed endless. The long list of ways to "fix" the energy of feeling bad in any way was long, but the ways were rarely healthy.

So, there I was with three days of better, healthier choices. I was making my bed, cleaning, getting to work early for every shift, and my conversations with my customers were more cheerful. I was talking with Bonnie all about the meetings and stories and we even had a laugh or few about some of our own partying nights back in the early high school days. We had some meaningful conversations about the level of honesty that I was witnessing, and my own honesty about the depth of shame I felt.

I was having meaningful conversations with these new friends, too. They were asking me how I was with great sincerity, and I was answering with honesty and vulnerability. I shared about feeling uncomfortable and yet also at home. I shared about how overwhelming it felt to consider the durations of clean and sober time they had, even those that were still somewhat new, with just thirty days or two months. The idea of not drinking or using any substances for that long was a bit surreal. I wanted to know what it felt like, and witnessing their example was very impressive to me.

I was also very concerned about them. I was invested in the stories and the well-being of these newfound friends. In many of the meetings, people would share about what was going on in their lives that was challenging. There were tears, often a lot of cussing, and overall, just real talk about navigating their lives and the situations they were working through without the use of any substances. There were also these moments of witnessing so many of them light up when they shared about how grateful they were to be in recovery, how their lives were improving, and how so many aspects of their lives were mending.

One night, a man covered in tattoos shared that after his release from prison, he got a job selling vacuums door-to-door. He borrowed money from a friend to buy a suit so he would look more professional. He smiled when he told us it was baby blue. His eyes shined as he admitted that his vacuum sales didn't go well, and he relapsed on heroin. He threw a vacuum across a field and fell asleep in the grass, still wearing the new blue suit.

As I felt how sad it was for him to feel this defeat, I realized he was laughing. Everyone was. I connected to that moment. The laughter was about relating and knowing that he'd overcome that experience. The laughter was about knowing you can experience these great defeats and feel so hopeless that you'd sleep in a field in a new suit, but get back up, face your demons, and keep going. It was about the very meaning of the word *recovery*.

Such moments were profound. I wanted to hug every one of them and tell them I cared and that I was cheering for them. While I didn't hug everyone, I did appreciate the amount of hugging that we shared. They were strangers, and yet they felt like very close friends in an instant.

This third-day realization was a quantum leap from the self-destruction I had been choosing daily for years to a fully awake soul that was very intrigued at this opportunity to do better, to be more like these people I'd just found in a smoky biker twelve-step club. I wanted to understand how they had light in their eyes and why they laughed when they told their stories of bad behavior similar to mine—stories that I hoped no one would ever know.

It was as if there was some kind of magic in the air. I was not only steering clear of drugs and alcohol, but I was a part of something special. They bared their souls to one another and to me. They opened a space in my own soul to show my own truths. I was connecting to the pillar that is community.

I was accepting my soul's truth of pain, defeat, shame, and hope for a better life. The elation of knowing that I was three days into making better choices, deeper honesty, and walking in a way that could truly change my life if I just held on to it was shining. There was a spark that lit in my own eyes, and I wanted to see it grow.

CHAPTER 14
Feeling Better

> *"INSTEAD OF RESISTING ANY EMOTION, THE BEST WAY TO DISPEL IT IS TO ENTER IT FULLY, EMBRACE IT AND SEE THROUGH YOUR RESISTANCE."*
> ~ DEEPAK CHOPRA

I WAS SITTING IN A MEETING during those first hazy few weeks, and I'll never forget it as long as I live. I don't know who said it, but it hit me right between the eyes. A guy said, "You're going to feel better."

I remember it being one of those moments where my ears perked up. I'm sure he probably added "For the newcomers..." before he said it, as I always knew I was supposed to listen when the word *newcomer* came up. I was not too fond of that word as I wanted to have two, three, or eight years of sobriety like so many who were obviously more comfortable in their skin than I was.

Then he clarified, "I don't mean you'll feel *better*. I mean, you're going to *feel* better."

I instantly understood. I was experiencing a great deal of emotion in my newfound recovery. I was scared, excited, uncertain, and yet safer than I'd felt in years. However, if you asked me to identify my emotions, the best I could give you is over-whelmed. The beginning road of recovery is not for the weak.

I didn't fully know the difference between fear and anger. I couldn't identify anxiety as anxiety; I just knew my skin was constantly crawling with nervous energy, and I was so restless. My mind continually raced with a thousand thoughts at a time.

Did I say the right thing?

Wow, she's so pretty. How could she be an addict?

No way, these people are clean.

I need a drink.

Should I be here?

I bet I could learn to drink normally.

I never want to drink again.

Oh my God. I just want to hug him.

I was so emotionally raw, and there was no question that I felt every emotion *better*. That's what happens when you stop numbing to escape every aspect of your life: You truly *feel* better.

As I reflect on these early days and months sober, I can say that while I quit numbing on drugs and alcohol, the depth of connection to the words shared in meetings became a deep need for more stories, more understanding of how they stayed clean, and more understanding of my own path since I was there, and I was feeling deeply engaged. One of the recommendations for newcomers is to go to ninety meetings in ninety days. I went to at least one hundred and fifty.

One of my favorite quippy lines about the twelve-step programs is that they're brainwashing. In response, not only have I heard it, but I've said, "My brain needed washing."

I craved relief from my cravings, and the only place where I felt even a slight sense of groundedness was while sitting in a meeting. Something in the energy of the rooms was truly comforting to me. It may have been the comforting smell of the coffee or even the cigarettes. It may have been how almost everyone in the room listened when someone spoke. It may have been knowing that I was not only welcomed to the club, but also genuinely wanted to be there.

Today, I know it as Divinity, connection to the community, and my own spirit. Back then, I could not have named it if I had tried. I was just drawn to the vibe of the rooms and the souls that filled them.

I listened to the stories of the destruction caused by addiction and alcoholism. I heard people speak with great vulnerability and guilt about killing someone and the prison time they had done and were still doing in their own souls. I listened when they talked about stealing from their mother or father, who had only tried to help them, and the hurt they caused to their families, themselves, and several people who should have mattered more. I heard them talk about the laws they broke and the lengths they went to get their drug of choice.

Then there was Cody.

Cody was a heroin addict. I liked sitting next to him in meetings. He was friendly, funny, and yet rather quiet. He didn't share too often, but he always asked how I was.

I pulled into the club for a meeting, and two of the ladies I'd gotten to know were crying and hugging one another, and I felt their sadness. I walked up and softly put my hand on one of their shoulders.

"Cody's gone," she said.

"What do you mean, gone?" I asked, thinking he relapsed.

I'd heard a lot about relapse and witnessed the sadness, powerlessness, and reality that it could be any one of us who did it. So, that was my first thought.

"He died. He went back out and he OD'd on heroin," she spelled it out for me.

My heart dropped, and it felt as if I turned white. I felt both disbelief and deep sadness immediately. I was really feeling every emotion that comes with the loss of someone that you care about. I didn't know him well, but they did. Many had known him for much longer, and they talked of his struggle to stay clean. They talked about how he was found in a gas station bathroom, on the floor, having just gotten drugs minutes before.

The image of him on that dirty floor haunted me and took me back to the moment I was unconscious, and likely dead, on a dirty bathroom floor. The image of the hurt and sadness in the eyes of my new friends deeply impacted me. I understood grief and named it. I felt sadness and knew what the feeling was.

I felt shame for how I'd minimized my own near-death experience and continued so recklessly. I experienced fear that this depth of emotion may cause some of his closer friends to relapse too.

Feeling better isn't easy. Escape by substantial substance use is. The grander scheme of feelings in this moment was broad, and my understanding of both addiction and recovery deepened in a split second.

I attended his memorial with less than two weeks clean and sober. I wore a black dress, and so did most of the other women. The men were in new, clean jeans, and many had on nice shirts or even sports coats. I'd not seen any of them dress up before, but this was life honoring the fallen. We showed up present to the reality of substance abuse.

I watched them closely that day and was in awe of the way they handled it. There were plenty of tears, hugs, and beautiful words spoken about their friendship with Cody. The entire experience deepened my connection to the community I'd found. It deepened my commitment and connection to the future I wanted to get to know. Mostly, it deepened my awareness that my drug of choice was alcohol.

I got deeply honest about the fact that, for me, it was the best drug for the job. The job was to destroy the hurt, anger, uncertainty, self-hatred, and a hundred other emotions I didn't know how to handle. While I did have some moments of fun along the way, the truth that alcohol made so many situations in my life more difficult was clear. Reflecting on those nights at the biker club house in Denver and how I knew heroin was a possible next level for me made it even more clear that I didn't want to go like this.

I've said this once already, but I'll say it again. Early recovery is not for the weak. A lot is going on emotionally and physically, and it's hard. It's painful to look at the damage you've done. It's difficult to start feeling all the emotions and not escape them. It's deeply conflicting to want to bravely face yourself at a very tough time in your life that you know, without hesitation, you created.

I knew the damage my drug of choice had already caused me, but the disease of alcoholism and addiction is very sneaky.

I'd had many moments where I questioned if I was ready for recovery or if I was in the right place for recovery in those early days, as the monkey mind of an addict or alcoholic, especially in early recovery, is mischievous and deceiving. I may have known I was in the right place, and my soul may have known it, too. But wounded souls have thoughts that can run (and ruin) their lives.

I was twenty years old and hadn't done anything to the degree of what these men or women had. I hadn't been to jail. I hadn't done intravenous drugs, and I hadn't slept under a bridge or in a field. I learned quickly that not having hit a lot of the same lows as many of these new friends had me classed as a "high-bottom drunk." Never mind the blackouts or the fact that my hands were still shaking from alcohol withdrawal. Never mind the self-hatred and clear knowing of my own heritage. My mind was playing tricks on me.

One evening, shortly after Cody's funeral, I was at Jennifer's place, the woman who was at the speaker meeting on my first day. She lived in one of the end units of Recovery Row across from JC. As we were talking, I shared some of my thoughts about not fitting in and being unsure about recovery. We'd spent plenty of time together since I'd been coming around, and she knew about my background.

"I'll be right back," she said. A few minutes later, she returned with Biker George.

Biker George was the man who slept in the field in his new blue suit, and he was an elder of sorts. He was well-respected, had one of the coolest hot rod Harleys, and his smile is something I'll cherish forever.

His presence made me take pause and sit up a little straighter. I looked up to him.

The woman said, "I wasn't sure what to say, so I got George."

He sat down on the coffee table directly in front of me and was sitting very close to me, with no smile. His piercing blue eyes looked straight into my soul, and he said this:

"Young lady, there are hundreds of other young ladies just like you who are suffering from this disease right now. Just like you, they are wondering if they have gone far enough down the road to hell. But if you decide to stay clean and sober, you are one of the ladies who will be here when they come in. You can tell them you didn't have to go that far, and neither do they."

I'm sure he said much more, but he had me at being there for others like me.

If there was any emotion I was sure of, it was how alone I'd felt being so young and out of control. I knew very few others my age who drank like me, and even fewer who wanted to stop and make a better future for themselves like I did. I knew shame, isolation, and confusion well, but support and connection were new.

His words were like an awakening to this vision of the many other young women I would meet in the days and years to come. I had no idea how intuitive I was then, but he was right. His words touched my spirit. They opened the doors to the pillar of connection, which is service work.

Shortly after that visit, I actively participated in the available volunteer opportunities. I spoke in meetings, led a few, and faced emotions of nervousness, anxiety, and hope. I honored the principles of responsibility, unity, and solidarity. I took a position on the hotline and answered many calls in the middle of the night from very loaded people or their family members who were desperate to help them. I connected with each and every one of them, facing emotions of both reward and powerlessness. I even learned some baby steps about letting go when someone I had agreed to meet in person didn't show up, despite our long phone conversation.

I sat in many leadership meetings with fellow volunteers and learned about the emotions of the ego and how they may directly oppose the soul's desire to help. I felt both irritation and a sense of grounded clarity as we navigated significant issues that affected the large area of Northern California we served. We were all volunteers, just making our way through one day at a time, learning how to feel better, help others, support each other, and stay connected as we tried to keep a good thing going.

I also got my first office job. I was hired by an organization that processed student loans for many state and federal programs. I started as a temp and was hired permanently within the first three months. I quickly learned a great deal about the industry, took pride in my work, and began to understand work ethic on an entirely new level. I was proud of my new role, which I felt elevated my station in the world. This was a significant shift from my role as a server in a diner to being a professional with a national organization that assisted parents and students as they navigated higher education.

Reflecting on this many years later is a sweet reminiscence. I learned a great deal about my emotions and how to manage them in a healthier way. It was deeply connected to my awareness of the spiritual principles that I was learning through attempting to work the steps, as well as witnessing the example of those who had walked them before me. I learned to navigate my compulsive and impulsive nature rather than allowing it to dictate escapism behavior.

I couldn't name the emotions I experienced then as well as I can now, but I faced them, I connected to each opportunity to walk through them, and I stayed clean and sober. I handled some of them terribly and some slightly better, but I didn't drink them away.

Service to others in both my professional and community roles was a powerful catalyst to the foundation that kept me clean, sober, and committed to a path of growth through acknowledging and facing my feelings. I was only beginning my spiritual journey, and the principles of spirituality and Divinity were a frequent topic of conversation, a community conversation when it came to managing life on life's terms and the feelings therein. We talked about which principles we were practicing in our everyday lives, such as humility, unity, grace, integrity, and several others. These were conversations I'd never had before, and all I could think about was how these new friends applied these principles in their lives and how I could apply the principles more aptly in my own life.

It was my first true introduction to and connection with spirituality. The phrase "power greater than yourself" was used often. I struggled with what it meant initially, but I realized I didn't have to name it. I'm eternally grateful for those who walked with me and faced their emotions clean and sober, too. This stage of my recovery was only possible through the connection with this community. *They* were a power greater than me.

CHAPTER 15
My Fairy Tale

"SOMETIMES, SOULMATES MAY MEET, STAY TOGETHER UNTIL A TASK OR LIFE LESSON IS COMPLETED, AND THEN MOVE ON. THIS IS NOT A TRAGEDY, ONLY A MATTER OF LEARNING."
~ BRIAN L. WEISS

I'D SEEN HIM AT A FEW PICNICS and at a dance or two. He was gorgeous, and I'd caught his eye too. He had long, thick, curly hair, olive skin, and the likeness of what I'd envisioned as Prince Charming.

I was behind the counter of a large church kitchen selling sodas and snacks at one of the weekend dances. He was there attending with his friend. I hadn't talked to him before. I was waiting for a break to see if I could at least walk by him and see if we'd make eye contact, but then I saw that he and his friend were headed toward the back exit door to leave. I'm unsure what compelled me, but I nearly ran to catch them. And this is what came out of my mouth...

"My God, you are gorgeous. We should get married," I said with a sly, flirty grin.

"I think you're gorgeous, too. Okay, we can get married," he smiled, but he and his friend then just kept walking.

In my delusional, impulsive excitement, I thought they were off to get the car and would come around to pick me up.

But alas, I hung out for another hour and then went home with the girlfriend who had brought me to the dance.

I was so excited that we'd finally connected and then so deflated that it was but a split second and nothing more than a flirtatious moment.

However, the following weekend, there was another dance, and he walked in. I watched him as he made his way to say hello to the friends he knew. He was in faded jeans, a Metallica T-shirt, and had on a black leather jacket. His long hair was curly and thick, and I was entranced. I wasn't sure how I would approach him, but I'd hoped he would see me and that I'd catch his eye again.

I was standing by a wall alone and just watching him and hoping he'd look my way. I was having a good hair day, wearing my best jeans, high-heeled leather boots, and a black Harley-Davidson tank top with flowers in the design. I was a little reserved because of the way they'd disappeared the week before, but I never took my eyes off of him.

The second he saw me, he walked straight up to me, stood very close, and began talking. He was taller than me and my head was right at the height of his shoulder when he put his arm on the wall behind me. I could smell his leather jacket as well as the scent of his skin, and the chemistry was undeniable. There was a degree of comfort and excitement in his presence, and I felt I'd known him for years.

He told me it was his birthday, and I was so honored that he wanted to be with me when all his friends were across the dance hall. We talked for at least an hour about my birthday coming in a week, where we were from, who we knew, what we did for work, music, and a million other things. Then he drove me home.

We sat in his truck and talked for another three hours in the parking lot. We laughed, we kissed, and we fell in love in that parking lot.

We would have talked all night, but I had to work the following morning.

For the next two weeks, we were inseparable. We joked about how we met and quickly agreed in banter about getting married before we knew one another's names. Then, impulsively, we drove up to Lake Tahoe, went to the first chapel on the side of the road, and eloped.

Our honeymoon consisted of getting tacos at a local drive-through.

He immediately moved in with me, and exactly two weeks later, I chose to stop taking the pill.

I'd been on the pill for years, and it's not supposed to be so likely that I would get pregnant in that first week off, but on day eight, intentionally not starting the next cycle of pills, I knew without question that I was with child.

We met, we got married two weeks later, and two weeks after that, I was pregnant.

He was in construction. I had an office job. We were madly in love and truly thought we had it all figured out. We struggled through the adjustments of our newness together, and we didn't handle all of the emotions well, but we were committed. We had so much passion, hope, and love.

We had the perfect plan, too. The job I had covered a six-month maternity leave, and he was an apprentice to a great boss who was training him to become a general contractor. His boss was working hard to complete the training as fast as possible so that he could pass his contractor licensing exam and make more money once the baby came so I wouldn't have to return to work.

We moved into a nice duplex with two bedrooms and set up the nursery with a pretty wooden rocking chair, a white crib, and some pastel animal print bedding and blanket sets. We didn't want to know the gender because we just loved the adventure of the life we were building. We laughed and cried about the excitement and the fear of being parents. We both craved chocolate peanut butter cup pie at the same time and ate far too much of it. We were in sync in so many ways, and it truly felt like a fairy tale.

I started my maternity leave from my student loan processing job a month before the due date, as I had a six-month leave option with the company that employed me, and I had had a terrible time sleeping or getting comfortable as the pregnancy progressed. Then, on the morning of July 12, 1990, just three days before my due date, I had finally found a deep sleep when the phone rang.

It was his boss, and his voice was shaky. I sat up on my elbow and tried to wake up fully. I knew something was wrong, but I was still half-asleep.

"Your husband is in the hospital. He fell off a roof," he said. "They think he broke his ankle, and he has to have surgery."

"For a broken ankle?" I asked.

"It's really bad. You should probably get down here."

I had gained far too much weight, I was sleepy, and every movement felt like slow motion, but I called my in-laws and made my way to the hospital.

When I got there and saw him on the gurney, I knew this was far more than a broken ankle. He was in excruciating pain, and the entire side of his body was covered in scraped skin. I sat with him as he fell into a medication-induced sleep while the doctors grappled with the extent of his injuries and debated the best way to operate.

They told me that he would be in the hospital for at least a few days, and I had an immediate sense of urgency to move into preparation mode for the birth, our home, and his recovery from this injury.

Being sober for a while, my intuition and instincts had grown sharper. I knew that even though he and I were both in shock, I had to consider what this meant for the birth of our child. I was due to deliver any day at a hospital in downtown Sacramento, and we were at a hospital forty minutes away. I had my file transferred to an obstetrician with privileges at his hospital in case I went into labor while he was there, as I didn't want to leave his side.

My instincts were spot on. His right heel was shattered, his left wrist was broken, and the surgery was going to consist of taking bone marrow out of his hip to put his heel back together. There would be a plate and five bolts in his foot after the surgery, which was going to take at least six hours. And, of course, I started having contractions.

I had only known him and his family for nine months, so the idea of facing birth alone became very real, as I wasn't comfortable enough with any of them to ask for help, and they were all stunned too, so they didn't offer. I called Bonnie, and gratefully, she didn't hesitate. She came to the hospital and became my chauffeur, birthing coach, and rock for the next two days.

By the time the contractions had worsened, my water broke and they admitted me. The monitors showed that the baby was in distress, so they didn't have time to do anything more than offer pain killers, as opposed to an epidural.

My plans to give birth naturally and medication-free were out the window. The only solace I had was knowing Bonnie was there. She was just as scared as I was, and we just held on during every breath and push.

Angelica Marie was born on her exact due date, at 4:02 a.m., July 15th, 1990, in a room about a hundred yards from where her father was in traction. I had only slept about five hours over the last three days, and the most beautiful soul I'd ever seen was in my arms.

We'd chosen names for a boy and a girl ahead of time, so at least this part was easy. Her name is in honor of my grandmother Dorothy Marie. The girl's name was based on knowing that by the time my child was old enough to understand the importance of my grandmother, she would be angelic.

She had had a great deal of distress during the birth, we both had, and we were both extremely exhausted. So, as soon as they were sure I had fully passed the placenta, and there was no immediate health risk, they placed her in my arms, minimally cleaned up, and I thanked Bonnie and sent her home. There was calm for the first time in three days, and Angel and I slept for the next four hours.

When we woke up around 8:30, they took her for a bath and to check all of her vitals. I was able to shower and then nurse her for the first time. When we were done, I stood, looked at her, and said, "You want to meet your daddy?" I stood up and slowly walked down the hall to her father's room. A nurse stopped me and said he couldn't have visitors because he had a slight fever, and they couldn't risk infection.

The emotion and tears that welled at that moment were unstoppable. "We have been through a lot. All of us. If you think you can stop me from introducing my baby to her father, just try." And I kept walking.

There wasn't a staff member at the hospital who hadn't heard the whole story, so she knew what I meant. She walked briskly in front of me, and with sympathy in her eyes, she stopped me gently. "Okay, okay... Just let me get things ready."

They put me in a mask, gown, and slippers, and I was fully covered from head to toe as if I were entering a hazmat scene. They also put a mask on Angel and wrapped her in a bigger blanket.

It was like a scene from a movie.

When we walked into his room, his leg was up in traction at the foot of the bed, his arm was up in traction in the middle of the bed, and he had gauze wrapped around his forehead.

I gently placed her in his good arm and said, "This is your daughter. We made the most beautiful baby in the world." I removed her mask so he could fully see her face.

He lowered his mask to make sure she could hear him, and he said, "I love you" with tears of joy in his eyes.

She smiled the biggest smile, and it truly took my breath away. While they say babies don't learn emotions that early, I will always believe that hearing his voice made her smile.

It was one of the happiest moments of my life. I was a mother, and we were a family. I've never been able to share about this moment without tears.

I learned later that day that our story had made the news.

However, it could have been better news. Our big plan for him to become a general contractor and for me to stay at home with the baby was drastically changed. I had no idea how much until a few days later.

I was set on breastfeeding. I'd read how much better it was for the baby's immune system. I'd been home for two days alone with her before he came home from the hospital, finding my way with a newborn, breast pumps, and how often I should be changing her.

When he got home, it was far more to care for them both than I thought it would be. He could not use the bathroom alone, could barely move, much less eat, and we had a newborn who developed colic.

I switched her to formula and spent the next four months choking down the fact that the plan we'd made was not changed but shattered.

I informed my employer that I'd be back to work, and we underwent the proceedings of a workers' compensation case for income, medication, and a settlement for the injury.

He fell because he and his boss were hurrying to finish a house before the baby arrived. In that rush, they chose not to use a harness to secure themselves on the rooftop, about twenty-four feet high. He slipped and fell, landing on a large river rock.

On the day I had to return to work, Angel was almost five months old. My husband was a bit more mobile with his walker nearby, and we'd been a good team through her first four months of navigating this change. He was sitting on the sofa, cradling her in his splinted arm. He had her little pink blanket over his shoulder and held her bottle in the other hand.

I'll never forget his "I'm so sorry" look as I stood at the door in my pantyhose, heels, and business dress, not wanting to leave them.

The emasculation he was suffering was beyond my comprehension, and I didn't see it. By my calculations, he would heal and return to work, and I would work until he did. We would get back on track in no time, and everything would be back to our little fairy tale.

But remember the manipulation and deceit that comes with addiction I mentioned? I had witnessed many slips with my peers in recovery, but I really didn't see his coming.

When we met, the only thing I knew was that we intended to live a life of recovery together. I had a blind trust that we would live out the rest of our days on our path of recovery as a couple, even with the many relapses I'd witnessed. I knew nothing of his prior addiction behavior or what might trigger him—until this point.

Within a few weeks of his surgery, he was abusing the pain meds. I knew the pain was immeasurable, but I didn't notice him abusing the pills. Honestly, I didn't want to see that as I was in full-blown working-mom-and-wife mode, with my sights set on a fairy tale reset.

Then came the settlement check.

It was a large sum of money, and the first thing he did was buy a motorcycle. Angel was just over a year old by then, and they were both walking now.

He started hanging out with some bikers I didn't know as well. They were in recovery but weren't in my circle of familiar people. I tried to be supportive, as he was coming back to life a bit. He had his humor and was excited to be riding and connecting with new biker friends and had also gone back to work.

We were still attending meetings, but we attended separately so the other could stay home with Angel.

We went on about our lives for the next year, and I saw the degree of physical pain he had simply walking. I understood prescription drug addiction but didn't want to even consider that he'd crossed that line. We had a plan to reset, damn it.

I had this blind faith in our marriage and future. I believed that we would make it through anything. But what came next was not something I was prepared for.

The bikers he was hanging with had been in talks for a few months with an outlaw biker club, not too unlike the one I knew and had spent a great deal of time with while in Colorado. He knew that an outlaw biker club often came with illegal activity such as drug and weapons trafficking, and often, violence, just like many street gangs. However, they all chose to become a part of that club officially, and it was a decision he made without any discussion with me. He was very dedicated to this idea of how this club was a type of family for him, and while I expressed my concerns when I did find out, I also knew that many of the new friends were in recovery, so I chose to back down and try to trust his judgment.

Shortly after Angel turned two years old, in late 1992, I started my career in the staffing industry. I was offered a job with Kelly Services. They were the original temporary agency and one of the most well-known in the world. I was elated. I found not only a great office job, but a career. And it was perfect for me. I loved people. I had really embraced the living a life of service, so helping people find jobs and assisting various companies across many industries felt ideal. It was a full-time position with benefits and an opportunity to advance that was very promising.

I loved the work, my boss, the team I was a part of, and the opportunity to work anywhere in the world with the organization. My husband was working, we were getting along for the most part, and life felt stable.

Until it didn't.

CHAPTER 16

Fairy Tale Versus Addiction

"YOU NEVER KNOW HOW STRONG YOU ARE UNTIL BEING STRONG IS YOUR ONLY CHOICE."
~ BOB MARLEY

IN JANUARY OF 1993, JUST A FEW MONTHS after starting with Kelly, my mom called to let me know that my grandmother was very ill with cancer of the liver and her lungs. She told me that they had had to put her in a nursing home. I'm not sure if I didn't fully grasp what it meant to be so ill that she had to do this, or if I was just in disbelief and denial. I had the mindset that she would get better, and I'd go see her once I had established myself with some vacation time at my new job.

Six weeks later, my mom called to inform me that I needed to get home right away and that she was buying me a plane ticket. They had moved my grandmother to my mother's house for hospice care, and she wanted me to have a chance to say goodbye.

I was devastated and simply full of bewilderment. I didn't see this coming. I took my grandmother for granted in a way that I can never repair. Being young, wasting so much of my time partying as a teen, and then running away to Utah and

California, I'd missed all of her end years. She and my mother had come to visit when Angel was born, and she seemed as normal as I had always known her to be. It was a memorable trip having to tote both my husband and grandmother around in wheelchairs when we were tourists in Old Town Sacramento, so I envisioned taking my family to visit her when Angel was older.

My new boss was a salt-of-the-earth woman who had asked me in my initial interview to tell her about someone I considered my hero. The first person that came to mind was my grandmother, so she fully understood the importance of my getting home to say goodbye.

Angel and I flew in on February 27th, 1993. It was late when we got to my mother's house. She and my stepfather took Angel to get something to eat and just be playful for a few minutes while I went into the room where my grandmother was lying.

I sat next to her and began talking. I told her how excited I was for her to see how big Angel had gotten and how I looked forward to at least one more talk before she left. The only response she was able to give was to brush her thumb along the side of my hand that was holding hers. I knew it was intentional even though she never opened her eyes or said a word. She knew I was there.

I went to tuck Angel in, and when she fell asleep, I went back to lie beside my grandmother. It was my favorite place in the world to lie next to her in peace and just ramble about life. I gently curled behind her, put my arm on hers, and talked to her. I didn't say much as I wanted her to rest. I looked forward to her opening her eyes in the morning so we could just love our time together as I said goodbye. I fell asleep next to her as I had done so many times as a small girl.

I woke up around sunrise and checked to make sure my grandmother was still breathing, something I'd gotten used to doing with Angel since she was born. I stood up and stared at her beauty for a moment. My gratitude for seeing her before she left, and even more, getting to sleep next to her for a few hours, was immense. I kissed her on the forehead and just let my tears fall. My heart was broken that it was ending and that I'd missed so much.

I went to check on Angel. She was peacefully sleeping and just so beautiful. I was lying there in all my emotions and sentiment, and I just stared at Angel, too. As my heart felt so heavy and yet so grateful, my stepdad came to the door and stood there. I felt his words before he said them.

"Honey, she's gone."

I was stunned. I had just been standing next to her not five minutes earlier, but I knew he was telling the truth. I felt it. A sense of peace washed through me, and I gently stood up and went to the room with my grandmother while Angel continued to sleep.

I didn't sit by her. I just stood at the doorway and felt the emptiness of the room as the tears rolled...

It was clear to me that she had waited for me, and overwhelming gratitude and honor struck me deep in my heart. The most impactful person in my life was gone, and the grief and guilt for not being there more in her final years was brutal.

I stayed in Colorado for her funeral and my boss granted me some advance time off to do so. I enjoyed being around the family for the memorial and there wasn't even one fight. My grandmother was a very loved and respected woman, and even though there were many tears, all towed the line of keeping it together in her honor.

When I got back home to Sacramento, something felt different with my husband. There was a distance, and I felt a disconnect. I tried to talk to him and work through it, but most of the talks ended in arguments, with his leaving.

Over the next few months of grieving, learning my new career, fighting a losing battle against my husband's new friends that he now referred to as *brothers*, I learned that he was trying to protect me from the life he was realizing he'd stepped into. The week I was away, he had had more time, and they pulled him into more of the "duties" that were a part of an outlaw gang.

He was a "prospect." This means that he was on the low end of the rankings among the members and had to earn his way up. He was given higher-risk tasks that were initiations into upper levels of rank, and much of this was very dangerous. He hinted enough for me to understand his risks, but he was also very nervous about saying the wrong thing, so he became more distant.

I'd gotten to know some of his new affiliations a bit. The two that he spent the most time with were initially good men, just as he was. They were in recovery, and I'd known of them from seeing them in meetings for a while. They cared about their wives and families. They shared valuable insights in meetings that I could relate to. They lived lives of service to others—until they didn't.

I don't know if it was sudden or if the denial was wearing off about what I knew his affiliation would likely lead to, but it was like watching a city burn, knowing the flames were too hot to go anywhere near it.

The seduction behind the illusion of power and the ego it feeds in that environment is scary and it seemed to implode overnight.

When he first started following the club orders, as all lower-ranking club members had to do, I saw the fear in his eyes about being around street drugs and guns and knowing that if he didn't do as he was told, he'd not only be kicked out, but they'd take his bike. As we started to disconnect after my trip to Colorado, I pleaded with him to forget the bike, as our family and recovery were more important. I felt his deep conflict about the decision, but no matter how hard I fought or tried to reason with matters of the heart, it was to no avail.

They won. The disease won. The seduction took hold.

We had a tough fight, and I packed a bag for Angel and me and stayed with my close friend Michelle. She was (and is) one of those friends who, if I even hinted that I needed some support, she'd give me the shirt off her back. She had a tiny one-bedroom cottage and moved her furniture to her garage so Angel and I could sleep on her living room floor. She cooked dinner, played with Angel to keep it as light as she could, and hugged me through endless tears once Angel was asleep.

The sleepless nights, the confusion of my little girl, and the heartbreak were an incredible load to carry. The disconnect between my husband and me was baffling. I missed the version of him that I truly believed was still in there but was lost to me. The grief of losing my grandmother and that I'd missed so much of her end years was eating at me too. In my first few years of recovery, I'd often said that if there were anything that I'd drink over, it would be losing my grandmother. I felt so overwhelmed with emotion, responsibility, and just bewilderment about the next steps.

He visited us at Michelle's often, and I let him, because he, too, was conflicted about what to do. I knew how much he loved us, and I had this hope that he'd wake up, give up the biker life, and we'd just go home again, with this ideal of a reset. However, my thoughts and intuition were also balanced with my awareness of how powerful addiction can be, and that he could slip into a pretty dark place and fall asleep just as quickly as waking up.

On one of his visits to see Angel and me at Michelle's, he asked me if we could take a walk. His fifth clean anniversary would have been the next day, but on our walk, he admitted that he'd gotten loaded on meth and was heavily abusing the pain pills.

I remember the shift in my soul. The teetering ended, and I knew he was heading to an unreachable place.

I wish I had trusted my inner voice, but letting go of a person I love—the father of my child, a soulmate with whom I have a deep bond—is not easy.

From this point on, the roller coaster was not a pleasant ride, but I'll share the highlights.

He would get clean for a few days, and we'd talk about him leaving the club over morning coffee and playful times with Angel. I'd see these glimpses of him as the man I fell in love with, and we'd get back together. Then, out of the blue, he would get loaded and disappear for days. I'd call around to ask if anyone had seen him. I'd wait for the sound of his motorcycle rolling up. I'd hold on to the belief that this was all just temporary and again, that we'd reset our fairy tale. The Dr. Jekyll and Mr. Hyde personas were both very intense. I'd forgive, be hopeful, and then be crushed and devastated. Sometimes, all on the same day.

I knew that I wanted Angel to have a sibling. I knew that I wanted my children to come from the same father. And during one of the stretches of hope, I went off the pill and got pregnant again. In retrospect, I see my denial, but I had this belief that his love for me and our children would be the thing that meant more to him than any drug or biker lore.

As you can imagine, a second pregnancy was not a magic marriage saver for the mess we were in. Regardless, I was madly in love with the little soul growing inside me. At six months pregnant, I came home to a note on the kitchen table with shaky handwriting that I could barely make out, but I remember these words: "It's time we part ways."

Being distraught for the eightieth time, I went to see him with some final pleas for our marriage and family. I walked up to his friend's home, and through the window, I saw him with another woman. I didn't knock or ring the doorbell. I stood there stunned and in complete disbelief. I honestly didn't think he could ever do something like this based on the love I so delusionally believed in.

The devastation of this kind of confirmation should not have been as soul-crushing as it was. I should have seen it coming. However, letting go did not come easily. I had a story in my head, and I was damned if I wasn't going to live it out. I had years of emotional growth to catch up on and didn't have the maturity to understand the need for self-honor or self-respect before this.

I did everything I could to try to leave the relationship. I pleaded with Michelle and my sponsor, Shonee, to make me stay away from him. I tried to make plans to transfer with my job to Colorado, but there were no jobs available. I had good benefits and a new baby on the way, so I hung in there for dear life.

I stayed on this ride for a few more weeks, and the toll on my own recovery kept increasing.

The pain of witnessing his soul fully disintegrate and my desire to save my family were in equal measure. The stress, trauma, bewilderment, and deep hurt were not feelings I was managing well, and the grief of losing my grandmother was something I was trying hard to just detach from. I was falling into a deep disconnect. I didn't trust him. I didn't trust myself. I was angry at God. I couldn't even hear my community or my mentor, Shonee.

I wanted to drink at it. A few drugs came to mind, too. I wanted to hold down food and maybe sleep through one night. I wanted to tell Angel it was all going to be okay and mean it. I needed to support the nourishment of my beautiful, growing baby bump without all of the heartbreak, hurt, and fear. Yet, I was falling apart.

The only clarity I did have was that I didn't want to do what he was doing, and I didn't want to dishonor the version of me that my grandmother knew I had become before she died. I knew that if I did drink or use any drugs to attempt to numb the emotions and disconnect from my disconnect, I would be no better than he was. I had a circle of friends beside me that was like family, and they had been through incredibly difficult times and stayed in recovery. Even though it felt distant, that connection was like a wind beneath my wings. I also knew my grandmother was watching, and I didn't want to disappoint her. I knew what I'd witnessed and experienced in those last few months with him was something I never wanted to do to anyone, not my children, not my grandmother's memory, not myself.

So, I didn't.

It was somewhat like revenge. I'll show you what it's like *not* to use. I'll show you what it's like to parent our children and honor my word. I'll show my grandmother that I, too, am strong and that I won't allow the chains to take hold of me again.

And while I know that's not really how revenge works, that's how it felt. The sheer anger at the disease of addiction and alcoholism saved my life from a choice that would have destroyed it. I know this because the destruction I witnessed based on his numerous decisions to use, drink, call me horrible names, and show up with drugs and guns on his person were all memories that haunted me for years. Having to tell him to leave in front of his crying four-year-old was deeply conflicting, but motherhood won over the broken-hearted wife.

These moments were some of the worst incidents of trauma I'd ever experienced in my life. Sadly, my gestating baby girl experienced a great deal of this with me.

On Saturday, May 7, 1995, at 6:35 p.m., almost a month before her due date, Raeanna Michelle was born. Just like Angel, she was absolutely stunning. The moment I held her, my heart as a mother grew ten times stronger than it had been just hours before. I'm sure my soul somehow knew what was ahead for my marriage and that it would need to.

Because this is often corrected, her name is pronounced "Ray-anna," and we often call her Rae. She was given her middle name after Michelle, who had been the most profound support a friend could ask for. I had no family in Sacramento and my in-laws made it clear they didn't want to be involved. But I had Michelle, a friend, a sober sister, and a beautiful light who walked next to me in the worst of times.

A few weeks after Rae was born, I was notified that our rent check had bounced. We were evicted because he'd taken the money for the rent out of our account, and I had four days to pay, which I couldn't do.

Gratefully, Michelle let us stay with her again. Just as before, she didn't hesitate to open up her tiny one-bedroom home to me, my four-year-old, and now, my newborn. She loved them and me like her own. She helped with meals, bottles, baths, and soothing tears for all of us.

I wish for everyone to have a selfless friend like Michelle. She held the line when I couldn't.

When Rae was four months old, a job transfer opened for me in Colorado, and I accepted it and was planning the move home with my daughters. Their father had been living with his parents and was clean again. He was kicked out of the biker club, and they'd taken his bike, so I agreed to let him help us with the move.

Believe it or not, we were trying again.

CHAPTER 17

Crossroads

"EVERY SO OFTEN, LIFE OFFERS YOU A RESET BUTTON. WHEN IT
DOES, YOU NEED TO PRESS IT AS HARD AS YOU CAN."
~ RILEY SAGER

THE TWO DAYS THAT WE DROVE the moving truck to Colorado together as a family were a very memorable and fun trip. We'd stopped in Reno and took the girls to Circus Circus. Rae was a baby, but Angel had a blast, and the light in my husband's eyes as he was with us and had a fresh start gave me a renewed sense of hope. I had a lot to forgive, but I had my little family, and I knew that if we just held together, forgiveness would come easily.

We found a townhome, and he accepted a local construction job. We found a few local meetings and tried to begin healing. However, there was a lot to overcome. I was deeply traumatized. Rae was extremely restless and ill. Being born almost a month early, her digestive tract wasn't fully developed, so she had severe reflux, colic, and could rarely hold down food. Additionally, my husband really disliked Colorado and was struggling with homesickness.

He got word about a job that paid almost three times as much as he was earning in Colorado at a construction site in

California that had just won a large government contract. We debated whether this was a good idea, given that he would be separated from us and exposed to his old influences, but we were also struggling financially. So, he accepted the higher-paying job and traveled back and forth between the two states. He stayed clean for an entire year and sent money to support us. He enjoyed his trips to Colorado to see us, and then he would go back to California, as that contract was at least another year long.

Then it happened again.

There is a common line among those in the twelve-step program of AA in particular, that "Staying sober is easier than getting sober." I know it may sound like a riddle of sorts, but what it means is that getting sober the first time is pretty tough. When you choose to face your demons of addiction, you are full of shame, fear, and the depth of emotion is heavy. If you choose to go back to substance abuse again, coming in the next time, or the next, or the time after that, is much harder than the first time because you've added more shame and less resilience. So, those of us who have stayed for long durations say it clearly that it is easier to fight through a bad day and stay the course of the mountain you started climbing from the beginning, than it is to fall backward and start the climb again with a heavier backpack.

There has never been a more relevant example of this than my children's father. His backpack was full of rocks, the zippers were barely holding, and one of the straps was broken.

I never knew what the slip trigger was, and at some point, no matter how much hope I had, I stopped caring to try to figure it out. Staying sober is something he simply could not do. He'd fought to get sober so many times, and then he'd get drunk or loaded again.

I'd gotten used to being a single mother. I'd been doing it long before Rae was born, and I'd been doing it while he was working in California. I'd gotten used to feeling shame for believing in him and feeling so deeply disappointed and let down when he broke his promises.

What I hadn't gotten used to was how to maintain my recovery in Colorado. I didn't have a community. I rarely prayed or connected within. My mentor was in California, and we didn't speak nearly enough. The primary role I had in service was as a mother. At that, I felt like I was failing. None of the pillars were stable in any way.

I had stopped attending meetings because I didn't like how they were conducted. I continuously compared the Colorado meeting experience to the experience I'd grown familiar with in California and made no effort to adjust to the differences. I judged and became resentful of too many aspects of my life, especially myself.

Being back in Colorado with all of the trauma of the prior few years, I picked a lousy time to stop focusing on my recovery. It would have been amazing if I were a normal person with average everyday problems, like needing to catch up on laundry or deciding what meal my kids would eat for dinner. However, I was a deeply frightened, hurt, lonely, broke, and traumatized mom who had zero self-care going on.

The disconnect hit a dangerous level.

It was a Sunday morning in late January 1997. My girls were with my sister at a sleepover with their cousins; their dad was in California, and we weren't speaking. I was in the final stages of acceptance that my marriage was in ruin. The awareness that my children would officially have a broken home was looming, and I was alone in too many ways for my own alcoholic nature.

Despite my children being one of the main reasons to maintain my recovery, thoughts of alcohol were seducing me. I was so far away from any form of spirituality that I was an easy target for the sneaky devil on my shoulder.

I drove to a liquor store that had been catching my eye on my way home for a few weeks. I pulled in, parked right in front, and stared at the door, then looked away and stared again. Initially, I didn't notice anything about the store, as I was in full-blown negotiations (and manipulations) with myself.

Your children will never know. No one will.

Your children need you. Go get them!

That first swig sounds pretty good right about now.

If you start, you'll never stop. What are you doing?!

You've earned this. The kids are safe. You can handle it. You won't be like him.

How could you even consider this after what you've been through?!

The angel and devil were going shoulder to shoulder, and then I saw it. The sign said, Closed on Sundays. I realized the lights were off inside, and I looked at the hours posted on the door again to double-check. It still said, Closed on Sundays.

I quickly realized the angel had won.

Then the tears came.

The reality that I was all too willing to give up almost nine years of sobriety hit me. I don't know how long I sat there in that morning's cold, but I couldn't settle.

I broke down. I knew I'd lost my way. I was afraid and angry and ashamed that I'd even had the thought of drinking. I didn't know how to handle the emotions, the responsibilities, the hurt, or, most of all, the abandonment. And there I was about to abandon myself.

As the tears soaked my cheeks and my sweatshirt, I yelled at God.

"What the fuck do you want me to do?! Seriously! Where the FUCK are you?!"

I opened the glovebox to get a napkin to wipe my face with. Moms keep a stash. And God might as well have said, "I'm right here, Honey."

The bright yellow AA meeting booklet, listing all of the daily meetings for the Greater Metro Area of Denver, was mixed in with the napkin stash.

I grabbed a napkin, slammed the glovebox door, and cried a little longer.

After a few minutes, the avalanche of emotions started to settle, and I knew what I had to do.

I opened the glovebox again and then the booklet. I chose a nearby meeting named Crossroads, started the car, and drove.

I arrived a few minutes late and was happy about that as I didn't want to talk to anyone. I wanted to avoid being greeted or introducing myself. I just wanted to sit there and hope to feel that familiar safety in a meeting of Alcoholics Anonymous that protected me from the disease of alcoholism.

I chose a seat at the back of the room, close to the wall, and tried to listen. I immediately found fault with the meeting, as I was one of the youngest people there. The meeting room was rented from a retirement community, and most attendees that day were my mother's age or older. So, clearly, I wouldn't fit in with *this* group.

As I fought to shut down my thoughts to listen to what was being shared, regardless of my judgment, I noticed the laughter and camaraderie among the members. It was clear they had known one another for many years.

Then it happened again. "I'm right here, Honey."

An old man with an oxygen tank was talking in a raspy voice. "Back when I drank at the Oak Alley Inn," was all I heard.

It took me back to when I was that little girl in the shack behind the bar. It took me back to my disdain for the Oak Alley Inn. And it led me to a clarity that if I didn't defend my recovery, I'd end up in a place exactly like that. I knew what version of alcoholism I had. I knew I had no choice but to rethink how I felt about meetings in Colorado. I needed to find a way to fall in love with recovery again or get used to the idea that I may be using that kind of childcare for the beautiful little girls I wanted so badly to show a different version of childhood than my own.

I must have looked like I needed to talk because someone asked me if I wanted to.

I struggled to speak while fighting back tears. I found the familiar and deep honesty that I valued so deeply in California, and I admitted to being in front of the liquor store earlier that morning, that I hadn't been to a meeting for a long while, and that I knew my recovery was in trouble.

While it was humiliating, I felt safe to be so raw. I felt at home among my people. That connection was present, and I experienced the familiar magic in the air I'd felt for years in California meetings. The age difference didn't matter anymore. It was comforting. In that single hour, the fear of myself and the disease of alcoholism disappeared like it had in so many other meetings in my early sobriety.

I don't remember who I talked to after the meeting, but I'm sure I did. I don't remember how I felt the rest of that day, but I didn't drink or use or continue crying. The familiar feeling of hope and connection came again. It was faint, but it was there.

I had digested the idea of my marriage ending, and the acceptance of my life as a single mom was making its very grounded way into my heart and mind.

Our divorce was final in March 1998. It was a five-minute court proceeding because we had nothing to fight over, since he was in a California jail. I had sole custody, full decision-making rights, a lot of debt, and a long road ahead.

But I was clean and sober.

I made a sincere effort to rebuild my recovery life. I went to several new meetings in the area and to Crossroads every Sunday.

The man with the oxygen tank, Ernie, had a cool indexing system for the anniversary medallions. On your recovery anniversary, he would give you a coin with a card that listed the names of all the Crossroads members who had carried that medallion before you.

I witnessed a former Denver weatherman accept a coin for his fiftieth sobriety anniversary. He often spoke, made us all laugh, and gave me one of my favorite quotes. "When your heart is full of gratitude, there is room for nothing else." (Dave Scott)

I befriended a feisty silver-haired fox, named Carol, who reminded me of my mother and what she would have been like if she'd ever become an AA member.

I met and developed a close friendship with a man who knew my mother from her Oak Alley Inn days because he had bought the place. I experienced the loss of this very dear and wise friend when cancer ravaged him and took him in three very short weeks.

I became a part of something again, and it was the connection to the community of this group that saved my life that Sunday morning. I was a respected member, a friend, and a woman who was pointed out when someone shared about the women in recovery whom other women should know.

Crossroads saw me through my divorce, a lot of single mom struggles, a few boyfriends, the loss of a job, the change of my career, the teenageism of both daughters, and many other wins and losses because there was a meeting book in the middle of those napkins that morning... and because I was supposed to be there and not drowning in a bottle. Because God is good, and he orchestrates just the right synchronicities and connections to save my life, especially when I'm not looking.

CHAPTER 18

"YOU CANNOT TRANSMIT WISDOM AND INSIGHT TO ANOTHER
PERSON. THE SEED IS ALREADY THERE. A GOOD TEACHER TOUCHES
THE SEED, ALLOWING IT TO WAKE UP, TO SPROUT, AND TO GROW."
~ THICH NHAT HANH

I FELT SO GRATEFUL to have a connection to my sense of self and to a community in recovery again. However, I knew that an important component of continued growth in my recovery path was to find a sponsor. As I mentioned in the introduction, a twelve-step sponsor, simply speaking, is a mentor. To most twelve-step program members, a sponsor is someone who has worked the twelve steps and has a strong application of the principles they teach, which they apply to their daily lives. They give their time freely to show how they worked the steps and, more importantly, how they apply the spiritual principles of the steps to their daily affairs.

Mentorship has been an essential element of success in so many of my endeavors, predominantly due to the depth of connection a mentor offers.

I've had mentors in business, child-rearing, spirituality, and recovery, and for me, identifying mentors that I respect, truly listen to, and apply their guidance has been tricky. I could have peppered all of the stories I'm about to share in the chronological timeline of the book, but I felt it would offer more clarity and poignance to share them in a full chapter that is dedicated to the process of choosing and working with mentors or sponsors in life. So, hopefully, my experiences will convey some of the wisdom I have gained and help you build guidelines for choosing mentors in your own walk.

I'll start with Randy. He was a very grounded soul who wore jeans and flannel shirts even in the summer. He had a long beard that he would constantly reach for to stroke, smooth and straighten when he talked. He was a close friend of my mother's, and he lived with us off and on for a few years when we'd moved back to Colorado. He helped with bills, handyman tasks, homework, cooking, and childcare, and was the only man I ever trusted in my youth. Our time with him was too short. He was a light-hearted soul who laughed a lot, and when he did, his shoulders shrugged. It still makes me smile just to think about that trait.

He had a presence that could calm any situation. I had no one specific lesson from him other than to try to make people feel safe around you, stay grounded, and to simply be a good person.

He moved away when I was eleven, never to be seen again, but the impression he left on me, my siblings, and my mother is one we all reflect on with ardor and fondness. I still aspire to hold space in a room the way he did.

Next, I have to share about my photography teacher, Jim, from my first semester as a junior in high school. He wore jeans and tennis shoes, unlike most of my other teachers. He had glasses and just a fun demeanor. He was a genuinely authentic teacher who cared about the kids, which was clear in the way he spoke to us. I not only had a few good chats with him but also listened to his chats with other students. He wasn't afraid to say it like it was, and he often put us in our place. However, he never did it with a condescending tone or a manner other than humor, heart, and a few impactful questions that made us think.

I only took photography for that first semester, but when I handed him the form to drop out of school, I could almost feel his heart sink. He was sitting on a stool in the corner of his classroom, and his whole body slumped as he looked at the ground for a long while, deciding what to say. "Are you sure?" He finally looked up. He was angry at my situation and knew that the path of a dropout is often a struggle.

I felt shame, bewilderment, powerlessness, and just the entirety of not being important enough to be kept in a stable home so I could graduate high school. "I don't know what else to do," was all I could get out as the tears filled my eyes.

He signed the form. I slowly handed him the school-loaned camera, and he hugged me. When he pulled away, tears fell down his flushed cheeks, too. I felt seen, heard, and cared for.

At that moment, I committed to doing better than the average dropout because I knew my success mattered to someone I had admired.

Next is Ben, one of the residential advisory staff at Job Corps. He looked just like Quincy Jones, or perhaps more like his uncle in his cardigan sweater. He was an older man with a swagger that made him just intimidating enough for his tough job, yet he always had a smile on his face that made him approachable. He worked nights and would wander through the dorms to make sure we were doing our cleaning, getting to bed on time, waking up on time, and he broke up a few fights, too. We had countless little chats on the dorm porch area, and he always had some wise saying or advice to offer to me and several other students. He was a safe, paternal-type presence for many of us, and that smile shined love on anyone he spoke to.

One night, I was up really late, listening to music. I had a set of headphones on with a long cord and was really jamming out. I was dancing and keeping quiet, but it was way past the lights-out rule. Ben walked by my dorm room, which had no door. At first, my back was to him, but in my peripheral vision, I saw him looking in as I turned. Then, he walked away with a bit of a strut to let me know he loved dancing too. He didn't say a word or stop and signal me to get to bed. He just waved like, "Keep doin' your thing."

People like Ben are rare. They allow you to be who you are.

At that moment, I felt trusted. He trusted that I was responsible enough to manage my sleep that night. He saw my spirit dancing and feeling some lightness, and in his way, he knew my spirit needed that.

Randy taught me that mentors hold a safe space for others, Jim taught me that mentors care about others' success, and Ben taught me that mentors allow people to be themselves. I feel really lucky to have at least experienced these examples of what it means to be in a position of authority, like a mentor, and not abuse that power.

When I first started my recovery journey in the twelve-step rooms, the prevalent message was to get a sponsor. I had an idea of a few traits that a mentor should have, and I assumed that everyone who agreed to be a sponsor would have these traits.

In those beginning days, it seemed that at almost every meeting I attended, I'd hear, "Go to meetings, get a sponsor, and work the steps." The only clarifying suggestion I heard then was to ask a woman if you were a woman and a man if you were a man.

My road to finding a sponsor had been rough. My first sponsor tactfully ended our agreement because of her friendship with my then-boyfriend's ex-girlfriend. My second sponsor ran group sessions that were more concerned with gossip than an effort to work the steps, my third sponsor simply had too much on her plate and was distracted in every visit we had, and my fourth sponsor insisted that *The Book of Mormon* be required reading for my recovery.

I understood the reasoning of sponsor number one. I had to do a bit of evasion to end with sponsor number two. I loved sponsor number three, but felt like too much added burden, and I left sponsor number four with a sense of respect that she loved her religion, but that it was not aligned with my path, so I could not agree.

By strike number four, I felt that perhaps the idea of a sponsor just wasn't meant for me. Honestly, I was disappointed, but I was still enjoying life sober. So, I focused on volunteer contributions. I had a connection to the gift of helping others in service. I had a connection to the community. I had a growing spiritual awakening through intentional time in prayer, and was connecting to a deeper sense of self, even without a specific mentor.

These were three of the four pillars of connection to some degree, not a strong degree, but they were present, and it was enough to keep me in recovery and not at risk of drinking.

While I was doing well enough, I knew that something felt amiss. I felt that it was likely the fact that I still hadn't worked all twelve steps. The idea of finding a sponsor and working the steps wasn't completely off the table. I just felt like I had to set it aside for a while.

I had a cool friend named Shonee. She had been clean and sober for a few years longer than I had, was close friends with all of the same biker friends that I trusted and had lived a lot of tough times in the outlaw biker life before sobriety. Her journey in recovery was hard-won, and her presence was forthright, beautiful, and came with the added bonus of a wicked sense of humor that I loved.

We attended many meetings together, and she became one of my closest friends. She knew about my first four sponsors and that I'd done everything suggested to manage my recovery except the steps.

In the heart of all of my marital difficulties, the hurt, anger, and confusion about life and recovery were mounting. I was at a meeting with Shonee, and I had shared. It was emotional and heavy. I don't remember exactly what I said, but I'm sure it was something about the struggle with wanting to drink and yet wanting to get through this really tough time without drinking for my children. Even though I typically tried to speak in general terms and not share too much personal detail, she had first-hand knowledge about my struggle with my marriage and how conflicted I was.

After the meeting, Shonee hugged me and said something sarcastic yet loving about my need to work the steps. I related to her more than anyone in my life then, and we just got each other. I don't know where the comment came from, but I said, "You know you're my sponsor, right?"

"I do! And it's time we get those damn steps done," was her very swift reply.

I was almost five years sober at that time, and while I had gained some tools to manage life in recovery, there was so much more that I would learn in the coming weeks.

Shonee balanced her loving presence and acceptance of me exactly as I was with a firm hand that only a biker chick with her brand of badassery can offer. And I paid attention.

She told me to get a sitter and come to her house on Saturday with a notebook and a pen. When I arrived, she sat me at her kitchen table, and we started the process of the steps: a lot of conversations, a lot of writing, and then more conversations about what I'd written. She poured coffee, wisdom, and countless hours into my recovery.

She had that beautiful mix of being an example of a good person, seeing the light in me, and helping me to see it, too. She genuinely cared about my success, my spirit, and my recovery, and she held space for me like I was her own family. All of those traits that I had so looked up to in Randy, Jim, and Ben were in this one beautiful soul, and I'm eternally grateful.

The connection to mentorship in recovery began with Shonee. She provided wisdom, support, and an example of how to live a healthy, authentic life, which I needed. I opened up with Shonee in a way that was honest and raw, and she not only loved me anyway, but she respected me for it. I learned that one-on-one connection with a mentor was a critical pillar in my walk of continuing to grow in every role I had and my life's aspirations. It became clear that I must share my deepest wounds, fears, joys, and accomplishments with at least one trusted person.

Our connection showed me what was possible by trusting someone I respected and aligning that with trust in myself to be honest, open-minded, and willing to face life's difficulties. This built a foundation of faith that I can and will always overcome the bad times, and I don't have to do it alone. Our relationship opened the door to the power of allowing myself to be led and guided by a mentor. For as long as I live, I will try to pay forward her love, wisdom, and sharp wit.

CHAPTER 19

Dorothy

"A GOOD EXAMPLE HAS TWICE THE VALUE OF GOOD ADVICE."
~ ALBERT SCHWEITZER

I MOVED BACK HOME TO COLORADO in 1996 and spent the next five years adjusting to recovery in Colorado. I worked three jobs, often four. I took care of my children and my home. I stayed sober, with only that one close call; I went to meetings, connected to the community of recovery, and found commitments to hold to a primary pillar of connection in recovery that I sincerely enjoyed, service. However, I was living in a state of deep stress, overwhelm, and still, the grief of my divorce.

Part of my struggle with the transition was that there was no Michelle or Shonee nearby. They had both been such supportive people in California, and now I was a single mom, working too many hours and struggling to find my way in Colorado.

As my contact with Shonee naturally waned because we were in different states, she encouraged me to find a new sponsor. She and I both knew that finding someone I trusted and respected could be tough. She'd set quite a bar, and my effort or initiative to seek a new mentor wasn't great.

However, here's what I knew: Those first five years of struggle with mentorship left something wanting that Shonee truly shined a light on. Before our work together, I was proud of my life with the facets of recovery and connection that were community, service, and growing spiritual awareness, even with the many moments of personal stress and chaos that I didn't process with a sponsor. But when I did process life and so many difficult navigations with Shonee's help, the parts of the path that felt pitch black and scary then had a guide with a magic lantern that could illuminate the way. So, while I wasn't excited about the idea, I understood the importance of finding a sponsor in Colorado.

Since very early in recovery, I'd heard the guideline "look for someone who has what you want." Over time, my clarity about what that meant sharpened. I sought to find someone with all of the qualities I'd identified in a mentor through Randy, Jim, Ben, and Shonee, but they also had to *have* what I wanted.

To the older and wiser version of me, this meant they were living a life I intended to grow toward. This meant they understood and lived in a healthy and stable relationship, carried themselves well, and were emotionally, spiritually, and financially secure. They had to be well-versed in the twelve steps, the principles they teach, and life in recovery as a whole. Of course, I also hoped to find a woman who understood motherhood from at least a similar perspective to mine. It felt like a pretty tall order.

Crossroads had become a favorite meeting and community connection that I rarely missed. I began to build a good rapport with the other attendees. I also attended several different meetings and began connecting with the communities there. I'd befriended many women in recovery and paid attention to whether they met all of the criteria I sought in a mentor. It's not dissimilar to choosing a life partner. You get together a few times and decide if the relationship has any merit or potential.

I had coffee and various conversations with many women. I paid attention to what they said in meetings and various personal traits, such as how they treated a server or kept their homes. I listened to how they spoke about other people and cared about how they conducted themselves in discussions about recovery. Many of them became friends, but they weren't what I sought in a sponsor. Call me picky, but I was pretty shaken by my lack of good choices in sponsorship in early recovery, so I didn't want to mess this up. I knew that a good sponsor was a critical pillar in my recovery, and I knew she was worth the due diligence.

However, if you don't continue the process of digging, complacency can become an enemy. I didn't take the search too seriously. I'd had numerous conversations about sponsorship and recovery and started to find fault with many of the women I was talking with. I had grown cynical and even a little bitter about how much effort it was taking to stay in recovery.

In 2000, I had a challenging situation with a girlfriend in recovery. She was close friends with a guy I was dating. Both of them often confided in me about different conflicts they had with one another and yet asked me not to speak to the other about these things. On more than one occasion, they each put me in the middle by either telling me how upset they were with the other, sharing too many details, and then asking me what the other said about the matter at hand. It was a mean case of triangulation that was simply a lose-lose situation no matter how I tried to navigate it.

One night, the boyfriend pressed, and I felt cornered. It wasn't a new occurrence, and it was always uncomfortable. I was conflicted and exasperated, and while I didn't share anything specific, he was able to read me. He knew that I knew something about her being upset with him. He asked pointed questions in anger about their situation, and I clammed up. By doing so, I gave away that she was mad, which she didn't want him to know at the time.

A few days later, I was invited to speak at a meeting, and my close girlfriend attended to be supportive, but my boyfriend didn't. After the meeting, we were walking to our cars, and in typical forward and honest fashion, I shared with her that again he had pressed about the situation and that I refused to talk. I admitted that my refusal to speak gave away that she was upset with him.

I reiterated that I didn't say anything specific, but she became very angry. While I tried to defend my repeated position of being caught between them unfairly, she chose to end our friendship.

I had not made many close friends in recovery in Colorado, and she was very important to me, so this was a devastating loss at the time. I felt like I had been set up to fail, and I did. I tried desperately to repair the friendship and defend my stance about being put in the middle, but to no avail. I was simply cast aside because this had happened before, and she felt I had betrayed her trust.

The effect on my mental and emotional health was one of complete isolation and withdrawal from any meaningful relationship or connection, including my boyfriend. I'm not sure if the isolation was intentional, but the idea of unconditional love that I had both taken for granted in many of my twelve-step relationships, as well as tried to practice, was deeply wounded. I continued to attend meetings, but I did so on autopilot. It was simply what I knew as part of my routine.

I found myself sitting in meetings and tuning out. I felt angry and judgmental about what people were sharing, as if their contributions lacked authenticity and true honesty. After these meetings, I left feeling irritable and discontented about recovery as a whole. The devil on my shoulder found his voice again, and I struggled with perspective, not realizing how much I was disconnecting. It was as if I had a version of amnesia that caused me to forget why I was in recovery in the first place. I even began to wonder if perhaps alcoholism wasn't my problem.

There emerged this seductive idea that maybe I was just young and immature when I got sober, and now that I was older, I could drink like a lady. I considered the thought of having a glass of wine with a meal and enjoying how it may pair well. I thought about having some kind of frozen cocktail with a decorative umbrella on a hot summer day. I considered what it would be like to have one or maybe even just two drinks and if I would be able to stop there.

However, one self-truth that I was in no denial of was that I had never, not one time, *wanted* to drink like a lady when I was in my drinking years. I wanted to drink heavily and find a significantly altered state as quickly as possible. While that seductive thought of being older, being wiser, perhaps being able to control my drinking with more society-based normalcy was present, my memory of being interested in nothing but oblivion as soon as I took that first drink went down was also very sharp.

My memories of defying addiction during my divorce were vivid. My honor for my grandmother was strong. I vividly remembered that Sunday morning when I found Crossroads. The reflection of the magic I had experienced when I applied the tools and suggestions Shonee had taught me, from which I'd gained so much strength, was sharp and gnawing at me to put them into action.

I felt a sense of fear and I knew that I needed to cut that lousy thinking off at its knees. I knew, with clarity, what my version of alcoholism was and is, and I got serious about identifying a woman who had what I wanted. Finding a sponsor and working the steps again became a priority.

Gratefully, she was right under my nose. She had been there since that Sunday morning when the angel on my shoulder won.

I heard it again. "I'm right here, Honey."

When I identified her and considered asking her about sponsorship, I kicked myself a little. I'd always looked up to her. I'd often laughed at her wit and sarcasm and felt she carried herself better than many women I'd met since moving home.

And want to hear something special? Her name is Dorothy, just like my grandmother's.

Dorothy had attended the Crossroads meeting for as long as she had been sober. She was in a healthy marriage to a man who was also in recovery, and they had a beautiful way about them that I admired. I'd heard her share her knowledge of the steps and many spiritual teachings in meetings. She shared in a way that made it easily digestible and acceptable to anyone who listened. She had no bias, just wisdom. She also spoke about many books on divinity and religion she had read, which gave me the sense that she had a diverse understanding of spirituality and was not single-minded. So, I asked her if she would be willing to meet for coffee, careful not to specify that it was to discuss sponsorship, and she invited me to her home for our visit.

When I walked into her clean, beautifully decorated home, I felt the comfort she had created. Her library loft was at the top of the stairs, and it contained hundreds of books and a comfortable chair by the window. I couldn't help but notice the love she had poured into making her home a place of hospitality for guests, herself, and her husband.

She had a beautiful set of cups and saucers that she used to serve our coffee (and cookies) with, and as we started talking, she had an air about her. She was both humorous and firm in the same sentence. It was clear to me that she also knew my real intention. I wasn't just there for coffee or to become buddies. I needed help.

She asked me some very pointed questions about how I was doing, such as what step I was on or how I felt about the step that encouraged daily prayer and meditation. She shared how she and her husband had a daily prayer and meditation practice together in the morning and how important it was to their partnership and their recovery.

I felt safe and intimidated at the same time next to her. She had all the qualities I'd sought, and I felt them immediately in our first meeting. She was gracious and far more knowledgeable than I was, and she hit every mark on the checklist of what I knew about mentorship or having what I wanted. I felt such a strong sense of connection that I not only let go of how adamant I'd been about pacing the process, but I also felt a sense of urgency to not miss the opportunity to ask her if she'd be my sponsor during that first visit.

She not only agreed but went to strike while the iron was hot. She was very swift to lay out one of her requirements for those she sponsored: a committed daily prayer and meditation practice. Having almost fourteen years of sobriety at this point, I had an understanding of the step that encouraged this, but not a committed daily practice. I had sporadic prayer and meditation efforts, and Dorothy was quite specific about the importance of this daily requirement.

I must admit that it took me several weeks to build this commitment, and the story of how I did it is also relevant here. It is what brings us to the fourth pillar of connection, daily divine alignment, and I grant this knowledge with gratitude and honor to Dorothy specifically, because it was her push that gave me one of the most treasured practices of my life today.

Dorothy and I agreed to meet weekly for the first six weeks to get to know each other and work on our first round of the steps. During our second meeting, she asked me how my daily prayer and meditation practice was going. I responded that I had prayed in the car on the way to work and with my daughters at night before bed, but it wasn't daily. She gently, but firmly, stated that this was worthy of creating a daily ritual and that it was essential for our work together to go well.

When we met again for our third meeting the following week, she asked me the same question. I mentioned that I had been working on the idea of this ritual, and I'd made time for it by getting up early three days that week. Again, she stated firmly, and not quite as gently, that I needed to honor this requirement *daily* if she was going to continue sponsoring me. The stern look on her face told me that if I didn't honor this part of the agreement, our next meeting might be our last.

So, I got on it. I created a ritual of waking, letting my dog Milo out, pouring my coffee, and lighting a candle to pray by. I went through a protocol that I had stumbled upon while at a barbecue with friends, P.R.A.Y. (praise, resentment, ask, yield). I sat in a chair that earned the name "the prayer chair" from my daughters. I listed what I was grateful for (praise). I asked for help forgiving myself and others (resentment). I asked for guidance on my thoughts and actions for that day and for blessings to be sent to all who came to mind (ask). Then, I asked to align my given free will with Divine will for that day (yield).

After five days of consistently doing this, I had a few epiphanies. The first was a deep sigh of relief, or deep catching of my breath, during the part of my prayer that was yielding. It was (and is) as if I felt the Divine truly enfold and fill me with light. I felt deeply connected to the Divine in a peaceful and supportive way, and my entire soul relaxed. I gained a deeper understanding of the meaning of surrender. Later that day, I also noticed that I was less stressed. I had a stronger instinct about how to handle things, and I felt more grounded and, more importantly, divinely *connected*.

That was in 2001; Dorothy has been my twelve-step sponsor ever since.

We've worked through the steps together numerous times with multiple intentions. We've worked through the AA steps and also the ACA steps, which is the program for Adult Children of Alcoholics. I gained deeper awareness, insight, and growth each time we did the steps.

We met for coffee or tea at her kitchen table and discussed recovery, our children, extended family, politics, the esoteric, careers, and, of course, daily prayer and meditation that I began calling quiet time. There was rarely a visit that didn't begin with "How is your daily prayer and meditation going?" We laughed, cried, and argued a few times. She usually won, as she was usually right. I witnessed how she lived her own life, and it was one of authenticity, integrity, and deep love for others.

I know that much of her example is defined by her development of her relationship with the Divine. She knows this, too, which is why it was an imperative part of our work together.

From the beginning of my journey with Dorothy, I felt as though I had increased the value of my recovery insurance policy. With the four pillars of connection to community, service, a mentor, and daily divine alignment actively in place, I knew that my path in recovery was more stable; more than that, it was much easier, more peaceful, and far more rewarding.

As my connection with Dorothy deepened and I honored my commitment to daily quiet time and divine alignment, a shift occurred in my connection to my AA community, and even more significantly, in my overall attitude and level of peace within. There was a new lease on life, and the alignment of so many aspects of my life truly came together in a way that felt as magical as it had in the beginning of my recovery journey.

Within a few months of consistent daily quiet time in prayer and meditation, I became aware of how much more insightful, intuitive, and grounded I had become. I knew, without question, that the majority of the shift had come from my commitment to setting the foundation of each day by aligning my will with the will of the Divine.

To this day, when I connect with Spirit and invite Light into my thoughts, my heart, and my soul, I feel a deep sigh of relief and truly sense the presence of divinity flowing with me and through me. It is a sense of knowing I am loved, supported, and guided. Those early months of experiencing this in my everyday life are what led to a stronger dedication to the daily ritual that I embrace so richly.

The gift of daily developing and fostering a relationship spiritually is something I treasure. My morning quiet time is a place I trust to bring all that I am. I allow myself to be truly held in a sacred place where there is solace, light, guidance, and on many mornings, tears. Sometimes they are tears of gratitude, and sometimes they are pleas for faith or trust when I have heavier emotions such as fear, anger, or sadness. This quiet space within my inner world is a place where I express my deeply sensitive soul, trusting that it is the safest place to do so. My relationship with the Divine has become the deepest and most beautiful relationship I have, and I know that's why Dorothy encouraged me to cultivate it.

My relationship with Dorothy and with Spirit taught me about the magic of recovery again, and magical things began to happen. That first year I worked with her, numerous women approached me to ask me to be their sponsor, furthering my dedication to the pillar of service. My capacity as a mother strengthened. My consistency with daily prayer and meditation became a nonnegotiable commitment and ritual that I genuinely looked forward to. Being grounded and having a sound mind was something I had not known to this degree before, and I attributed all of this to my relationship with and the example set by Dorothy, which alone was enough to keep me in line, but being close to her as we have been is an honor that I know, without hesitation, saved my soul and gave me great discernment when the voices of recovery (the angel) versus addiction (the devil) whispered.

So, as I share all of this with you, I hope you walk carefully on the path of becoming a mentee to a soul who has what you want, that you admire, and that you are inspired by. I hope you walk beside their spirit and learn what motivates them and how to translate that into what motivates you to live a life you are proud of and at ease with. Spiritual mentorship of this caliber is a truly critical pillar of connection. For those of us in recovery, it is invaluable. A relationship with a soul that is deeply connected divinely and wants to share the wisdom of that connection will light up your life in a way that is beyond magic; it is miraculous.

Chapter 20
Amends and Forgiveness

"Not everything that is faced can be changed, but nothing can be changed until it is faced."
~ James Baldwin

As I've written this book, I've had a great deal of reflection on what recovery really means. When I first stepped on this path, my main goal was to learn how to drink without blacking out or becoming volatile. I didn't expect that I would completely end my substance abuse. I didn't want to become spiritual or sell sodas at dances. I didn't want to sit in a meeting, hoping and waiting for that person who called the hotline the night before to show up. I most certainly didn't want to look at all of the wounded parts of my soul and take any steps (pun intended) to heal them.

However, I eventually realized that recovery means truly amending your life, body, mind, and soul, which is how to break the chains of addiction or alcoholism. As we have explored connection throughout the book, amends are like reconnecting the threads that have been damaged in a beautiful, hand-woven blanket.

The magic of waking up with a clear conscience is part of the path to recovery from addiction or alcoholism. Being there for others when they are new, confused, or have been around for a long time and are hurting is part of the path. It is also about being there for family, home, partner, or career, and simply showing up with a clear head. It is holding your feet to the fire of ownership for your actions and your healing. All of these are recovery, and all of these are part of the amends process. An apology is an action that is a part of that process, but it is only one action. Amends is *the* process of recovery.

Walking this path is not something I could have even begun to understand as the fog was just starting to lift. I was years into my recovery before I grasped some of the very simple basics of life that recovery through the four pillars of connection had taught me. Building a community, committing myself to service, learning from my mentors, and practicing daily divine alignment helped me gain the clarity, courage, and wisdom to make amends in my life. I was years into walking this way before I truly realized the extent of the amends I had made simply by making better choices.

From my perspective, there are three forms of amends that will paint a thorough picture of the process. There may be others, but to clarify the message, let's focus on these three.

The first form of amends is likely the most obvious: repairing the offenses to others.

When I initially began the steps, I knew that part of the process was apologizing and making amends. During this part of the process, I was encouraged to list the persons, places, or institutions I had harmed and make amends to them all (unless doing so would injure myself or others). I thought I had to apologize to all the people I had hurt. The thought was frankly nauseating as I'd embarrassed the hell out of myself enough, and I felt like I'd apologized (almost) daily for all the years that I drank. And my list felt very long. There were offenses to people whose names I didn't even know. There were people I was detached from. There were places and institutions, like Colorado or California, and their laws, that I had harmed, and I had no idea how to apologize to them.

Luckily, it wasn't *just* about an apology.

Here are a few examples of this and how each is as complete as it can be.

First, let's talk about Jeffrey. There is so much packed into the damage I did. Not only was I a horrible big sister to him when we lived at home together, but I left him when he was only fourteen. I had zero regard for his feelings or his isolation when I left. I had no idea that he looked up to me in some sense. I just escaped physically and metaphorically as often and quickly as possible without looking back.

In late summer of 1994, I took him to lunch while visiting Colorado. I had lived away from home for about eight years at the time. He was officially on my amends list, and I was making my way through each humbling exchange of the amends process as prescribed by the steps. At lunch, I fumbled my way through an apology for my behavior when we were younger, completely skipping over the fact that I'd up and left home without a thought for the effect it had on him. The conversation was awkward and uncomfortable, and he told me he'd gotten over all of that years ago.

I was relieved to hear it and felt a sense of being forgiven. However, fast-forward a few more years, after I'd lived back home for a while. He seemed distant when I saw him. He was curt in his responses and often very sharp. So, I called him one day to ask if something was wrong, and he blasted me. "You think you can just move home, and it makes it all okay? You left me! You left me alone with our crazy mother and couldn't have cared less how I was for years."

And you know what? He was right. I didn't care about him or how he was. I cared about myself and staying out of trouble and away from the substances that had taken me to dark corners. I lived in great fear of returning to Colorado and of ever feeling how I had felt in the multiple homes he and I had lived in.

It was a stark awareness of the difference between apologizing and making amends.

This conversation offered profound growth in my understanding of amends versus apologies. Once I had this awareness, I told him that he was right and that I knew now how my leaving had affected him. I apologized for my selfishness and told him that he had the choice to forgive me and give me another chance to make it right and be there for him from that point forward. I told him I was willing and wanted to be there for him, but that was all I could do. I had to allow the choice to be his from there, no matter how much I wanted to be forgiven.

I can't say that this road with him has been easy. I can't change the past. Older siblings leave home, but I was more to him than just an older sibling. I was a safer soul in his life than my mother was, even in my own dysfunction. So, my leaving him to find my own way left a void. I couldn't see it as clearly then as I did once I apologized. My willingness to make it right was and is sincere. We both lead very full lives, and we still talk, but our relationship is a work in progress. We do care about what happens in one another's lives, and that means a lot— hopefully, to us both.

Secondly, let's talk about Brook, the girl I'd physically fought with. This is a matter that needed a sincere amends, but it didn't occur to me until I was twenty-three years sober. And when it hit me, the guilt was immense. How could I have gone twenty-three years and not acknowledged this particular soul that I had been so intentionally cruel toward?

One day, I stumbled upon the MySpace profile for Brook. The memories of our exchanges, our fight, and how unkind I had been flooded my mind. I had said and done awful things to Brook, and in that time of unhinged and wounded youth, I felt fully justified because of the hurtful words she'd said to Izzy. My cruelty was in the name of protecting my friend, as well as my immaturity. However, it was in no way justifiable as a woman in recovery who was truly holding herself accountable.

As I reflected on those years and that particular dynamic, I was bewildered as to why I hadn't sought her out to make amends sooner. The only reason I could think of was that I didn't think I'd ever see her again, and I certainly didn't know how to find her—until now.

On her profile, I saw a beautiful woman my age with beautiful quotes and images. Much of what she shared aligned with my own beliefs. I saw similarities that I had not even attempted to see all those years ago in high school.

I wrote and sent her a letter through MySpace. It was as sincere an apology as I could make. I addressed my behavior and expressed my remorse for it. I shared that if the option were ever available, I would try to make it right.

And she wrote back! She suggested meeting for dinner so we could speak in person, to which I readily agreed.

A few days later, when I arrived at the restaurant, she wasn't there.

I nervously waited and waited, wondering if she was going to stand me up. When she arrived, I could tell that she was shaken and that she had been crying. She sat down slowly, and I sat still for a moment. I was afraid to say anything, but the silence was awkward, so as gently as I could, I said, "Thank you for coming."

She nodded, and I could tell she was fighting to keep it together. In a shaky voice, she admitted that she was afraid to come, and that she wasn't sure if she could be around me.

I had hurt someone so badly that almost three decades later, she was still afraid of being around me.

The guilt I felt in that moment is something I'll likely never live down.

I thought about our letter exchange and that she knew I had remorse. But as we sat there, I knew I had to say the words to her directly. It was important to me to look her in the eye and honor her bravery for showing up and allowing me an opportunity to apologize in person.

"I truly am sorry for all the harm I caused. I'm so sorry that I hurt you and put you in this position to be afraid to even be near me. I promise I am not that person anymore."

The energy never really settled. We made it through an appetizer, or maybe it was just an iced tea. I just remember that it felt very brief. The exchange left me feeling the familiar shame and inadequacy I had known much of my life. My hope to repair the damage I had done felt futile, and I questioned if I had caused more harm by trying to do so.

I attempted to connect with her a few other times, but it fizzled out. She never said any final words, but I knew she didn't want to allow the repair or become friends. I understood, too. Not every wound can be healed. I am grateful she allowed me to at least express my intention to do so, but I honor and accept her decline. The only amends I can make now are about how I live my life forward, choosing not to ever intentionally cause harm to another soul again.

Then, of course, there is Bonnie. She witnessed the ugly side of my behavior from a front-row seat. I truly thought I'd lost her a couple of times because my behavior was so bad. She had heard a ton of those repeated apologies that, at some point, became empty and meaningless words.

She also saw me, through very cautiously optimistic eyes, begin to honor my word and show up for my life and our friendship in a new way. She saw me come to many realizations about how much healing I had to do. She saw me start a career and earn promotions. She was with me the moment I became a mother, literally, and watched me raise my children with diligence, responsibility, and as much love as one human can offer another. She has seen recovery through the amends of living a better life. To this day, we talk about some of the dumb things I did, like eating her mom's leftovers when I was drunk, and how I can never amend that. We even dare to laugh at some of it now because so much has been made right. (Although I often wonder if sending her mom some kind of takeout might do the trick.)

As for places or institutions such as Colorado or California, turning myself in for drunk driving or speeding (often) was not something that would have likely been taken seriously as confessed to by a clear-minded sober person. The amends here were to (try to) stop speeding and not drive drunk. These are living amends. I've aced the not-driving-drunk one.

The second form of amends is to self, releasing shame and reclaiming integrity.

It goes without saying that one of the people we harmed with substance abuse was ourselves. There is self-abuse, self-neglect, and self-sabotage. However, when we step onto a path of connection and recovery, we become willing to live in a way that offers self-care, self-honor, and self-love. Forgiving the mistakes and ruins of our past is part of this; for many of us, it is a lifelong journey. We acknowledge that we cannot change the past, and we consciously make choices that align with our values and principles, guided by a sense of grace and diligence.

The most active living amends I make to myself involve being intentional about not placing myself in situations that could harm myself or others. I don't abuse any substances, so I'm not affecting my physical or mental state in that regard. Because I am clear-minded, I am more aware of my choice of words, thoughts, and actions. I have not perfected never saying or doing the wrong thing, but I am certainly more capable of considering each choice carefully to avoid causing harm in any way. All of these are also components of honoring my purest intentions to avoid harm to myself or others.

The third form of amends to consider is a bit trickier but truly important: forgiving others. In a way, it is amends to the self, part b.

I've processed a great deal of resentment toward my stepfather, my mother, and my roots. While I clearly remember there being injustice, violation, and harm, I have moved to a place of peace by releasing and forgiving many layers of this. This journey has involved significant healing work and has brought me clarity on how to live my life moving forward as an adult, mostly by understanding what I hope not to do. Additionally, it has lifted an emotion that for centuries has been referenced by many wiser souls than me as *poison*—resentment.

I'm sure you've heard the quote, "Hurt people hurt people." When I consider the extent of the hurt I may have caused because I was hurt, as well as the forgiveness I have had to grant myself, it has led me to a much deeper understanding of the pain that those who harmed me have carried. It has afforded me a broader perspective on why they may have hurt me and a deep level of freedom in letting them off the hook. It doesn't mean I forget; it means that I release and keep myself walking with clarity to avoid putting myself in harm's way with them again, but I don't allow it to reside in my soul either.

As you read this, I hope you sense a sincere willingness to amend/recover what I can and, even more, a sense of redemption for what has been recovered. However, I know there are limits to this. I can't turn back time; I can only move forward from this moment. I can't force anyone to accept an apology or amends; I can only express my willingness. Knowing that I have done all I can to the best of my ability has to be enough in these scenarios.

I strive to live a life of integrity and not repeat past mistakes. Just as I felt on that third day sober, today my conscience is as clear as it can be. I haven't always had a clear conscience since I found recovery, but I embrace this way of life for the vast majority of my waking hours. I'm nowhere near perfect, but if intention counts, I know in my heart that I have no desire to harm, manipulate, or slight anyone in any way. When I envision a beautiful hand-woven blanket, it has colors of integrity, forgiveness, humility, and love naturally woven into it. I pray that these are the colors that "cover" my path every day of my life.

CHAPTER 21

Paying it Forward

"HOW WONDERFUL IS IT THAT NOBODY NEED WAIT A SINGLE MOMENT BEFORE STARTING TO IMPROVE THE WORLD."
~ ANNE FRANK

WITHIN TWENTY SECONDS of hearing her speak, I knew it was her.

"My name is Marlena. I'm an alcoholic," she closed her eyes, shook her head slightly, and looked down as we all patiently allowed her a breath.

Then it came out. "I hate saying that! I'm twenty-one years old and have no business being here in this meeting. Who, at twenty-one years old, who hasn't been to jail, hasn't gotten a DUI, and is paying her bills on time, has to go to fucking AA?!"

She was on the verge of tears as she continued to vent her anger and frustration. Several of the people who knew my story started looking at me like, "This one is here for you, Paula." And I just kept seeing Biker George's face across from mine as he sat on that coffee table, so worried about me and so sure she would show up one day.

I was eleven years sober when I finally met the young lady that George told me about when I was so new. It's a day I'll never forget because it was a bit surreal.

There she was. I knew this was who he was talking about. I knew her story better than she did, as every word she said had run through my mind when I first went to meetings. As grateful as I was for my newfound recovery, I also remember feeling like I'd been cheated somehow and how I'd wished I could just go out and enjoy drinking like other twenty-somethings rather than sitting in AA.

After the meeting, we talked, and I told her we had some things in common. I shared all of the same points she was disputing and said that once I truly realized that my age had nothing to do with it, I'd lived the best years of my life.

I sponsored her through her first round of steps and have been a part of her circle of friends and family for over twenty-five years now. We celebrate sober anniversaries together, even if it's just a call or text exchange. We show up for family celebrations, like our children's birthdays or graduations, and we simply have this kindred soul sisterhood, knowing we both walked similar paths of getting sober at a younger age than most. We cherish and hope to never take for granted the bond we share. We are both very grateful to say we are still sober, and I'm honored to call her a dear friend.

This chapter is dedicated to a deeper component of the pillar of connection that is spiritual service, which is the true foundation of my life. I wouldn't have grown to understand any of the other pillars with as much clarity if it weren't for this one. This particular part of the path, paying it forward in service, has been paved with more honor, reward, and fulfillment than I can adequately express here, but I'd like to try.

When I started the journey of recovery in 1988, I was immediately curious about how these people who told incredible stories of lives almost destroyed by addiction and alcoholism stayed clean and sober. I was ever amazed at how light they were. They laughed and had an air of confidence that was starkly different from the stories they had shared about their active addiction days. That curiosity has never left me. I know today that they were light because they knew their deepest trials and wounds had value, as evidenced by their example of overcoming them.

Since then, I have learned of numerous programs, practices, and ideals that people have used to recover and heal their lives from the ruin that addiction can cause. While the twelve-step program and the principles taught and practiced therein remain a very prominent foundation for my personal recovery, I am aware of and respect many other approaches people have used to maintain successful recovery from addiction or alcoholism.

Now, there is one thing that all of these various recovery paths have in common.

By now, I would bet you could guess what it is.

Yes, connection. Connection to others they relate to, connection to others that are willing to help them, connection to those they can help by their example, and connection to a power greater than themselves. In the programs that I have explored, these are all components of success.

My personal experience with connection began with my witnessing of it on that first day, but it was more deeply expanded during the first ninety days of my recovery. It stemmed from numerous in-depth conversations and the sharing of wisdom and experience during the meetings. It came from witnessing the true freedom of laughter exchanged among friends who were very authentic and honest with each other as they shared inside jokes. It was the experience of relating to their pain, hopes, and sometimes sheer grit to get through a tough day. Most of all, it was the sincere love and concern for one another's well-being that captured me from the first moment I witnessed it.

I gained a new willingness to consider Divinity, and the many seeming coincidences that led me to this life in recovery. I went from a life of isolation and self-degradation, believing that I was not worthy of anything good, to an awakening that life could be gratifying in merely days. I attribute that to the connection to a community unlike any other I'd known, and I felt that in so many ways from the very beginning. Being human, of course, I've had moments of isolation or disconnect, but returning to and working to maintain the many aspects of connection I've shared in this book remains the road to recovery that fulfills and guides me every day.

The path of paying it forward is an honor that I didn't see coming when I began this journey, but it is what has fed my soul, filled my cup, and kept me growing for decades now.

Since 1988, I've sponsored many women, most of whom I began working with after meeting Dorothy, and I've done my best to follow the example set by her and Shonee. I witnessed the example they set in the community, and I try to emulate that. I speak often about solutions rather than problems. I speak of the power of daily connection to the Divine to anyone who wants to hear it. There are times when I use humor or even sarcasm to bring light to a moment that needs it. I sit with beautiful souls who are in deep pain and listen when they need an ear or offer my experience, strength, and hope if that's what is called for. I hold them while they cry. I let them yell and cuss and vent. I walk like those who have walked before me to the best of my ability, and it is a walk I treasure.

I've sponsored many women and guided them through the steps. Many have become close friends. I learned the deeper value of a circle of sober sisters with different durations, experiences, and wisdom in recovery. We all contribute many perspectives, and it has made for such a meaningful and rich love for these relationships. We are the ones who are there for each other, merely because someone was there for us.

One of these women lost her sister to alcoholism. When I got the call, the only thing I could do was immediately drive to be at her side. We sat in her car and talked, cried, and digested the news together. I don't know how long we sat in that parking lot, but I could not leave until I knew she was settled enough to at least get home and make some of the family calls she had to make. It was instinctual to be by her side, and an incredible honor that I was the person she called, knowing and trusting that I could hold this space with her and be there for her. We often speak about this moment that bonded our relationship forever.

Then there was the woman who was pregnant with her first child, and her husband had returned to active addiction through the use of prescription pain meds. I knew this experience all too well, and having twenty-twenty hindsight, I was able to walk alongside her as she navigated childbirth, divorce, and single motherhood. It was a powerful experience in paying it forward that is imprinted in my mind as to why I went through it first.

One of my closest friends, whom I had previously guided through the twelve steps, lost her daughter. It was one of the most devastating and difficult times I have ever had to witness and support someone through, but there was not a call unanswered, a breakdown that wasn't held, or a moment of remembrance that I don't honor as someone she trusts to carry this with her.

I can't count the number of calls I've received—from not only those I've mentored but also those who love them—to talk them off the ledge of breakdown, hopelessness, fear, anger, or even suicide. Having been through so many incredible experiences of each of these in my own walk, and, more importantly,

213

knowing what it is like to get to the other side of them, always has an incredible meaning as they settle, get clear on next steps, find hope again, and we end one of those calls.

With each of the souls that I have served, my message of connection is always the root of what I support them with. I am deeply clear that connection offers healing for the soul. Of course, where there is room to express all four pillars of community, mentorship, daily divinity, or service, I will offer them as a means to build a healing path that is sacred and unshakable. It is my experience. It is proven. The stability these pillars have provided is beyond any I've otherwise known.

As I've shared the stories in this book, I've used the word *magic* many times. I can think of no more fitting word to describe the power of having someone walking beside you on a healing journey who reflects you or your message. They can heal an issue because the mentor/sponsor healed it before them and showed them how it was done. The reflection of that awakening and shift in persona is incredible to witness, and it is deeply rewarding to know that a specific and personal experience contributed to it.

When I see them engaged in community and know they feel that unity, I trust they will build a deeper path of healing. When I see them connected to a mentor and following the path that the mentor walked before them, I know they will grow. When I see the grace in their manner and hear them speak of their relationship to the Divine, I know they understand the practice of daily divine alignment. When I see them reach out to another soul and that soul takes their hand, I know they, too, are as honored as I am to serve in any way they can to pay it forward. I know that my journey, my lessons, my love for these four pillars have been passed on, paid forward, and have created a stronger foundation for all of us.

Healing together allows us to become equals. It enables us to hold each other accountable as we grow, allowing us to better identify misaligned aspects of our spirit's light, because that's how life, growth, and healing all work. We ebb and flow.

Reflecting on myself through others I've supported has been very enlightening. My desire to be my best, do my best, and continue growing is much higher when I offer to help someone else do the same. I stay motivated, open-minded, and curious, rather than resistant, complacent, or worse, disconnected.

Working with amazing mentors and other wise souls who have done their own work before me through these many decades of learning and healing has been so enriching. Through their examples and my relationships with so many of them, I've developed my own wisdom as a mentor. I have walked with those who stayed clean and sober through the steps of AA, NA, and ACA, respectively, on their path. I've mentored women in business, motherhood, and one young woman through her youth when she was an at-risk teen in high school. In 2007, I stepped onto the path of becoming a therapist and took the support of others to an even higher level. It has been a very progressive path, and it is what earnestly led me to the desire to write this book and share my experience.

Being of service in a way that supports an individual's spiritual awakening, growth, and greater self-love is a profound honor and a role that brings great fulfillment, embodying the essence of paying it forward. Growing into an awareness of how the four pillars apply to this spiritual awakening and growth is now a message that I share with those I mentor, serve professionally, or anyone who allows me the opportunity to share this wisdom.

CONCLUSION

Full Circles

"THE PRIVILEGE OF A LIFETIME IS TO BECOME WHO YOU TRULY ARE."
~ CARL JUNG

WRITING THIS MANUSCRIPT HAS BEEN one of the most dedicated efforts in my lifetime to share my experience, strength, and hope with others. There are many other stories I wish to share, and I hope to do so in many different manuscripts that I've envisioned. I hope to have them on paper soon, but more importantly, I want them to support you, inspire you, and lead you to a life of contentment, fulfillment, and security that you trust.

When I got picked up hitchhiking all those years ago, I could have never imagined my life today. In my most honest moments, I didn't think I would make it past the age of twenty-five with my reckless and self-harming choices. But somewhere above the trees overlooking the patio on that gray Sacramento morning, I was heard, I was led, I was held—and I was loved. I've known that since 1988.

As we conclude this book, I'd like to share a few stories that have come full circle on this journey. I've shared so many of my ups and downs. I've shared about many lessons and people, and I wanted to round it out to show the true power of how the four pillars of connection have aligned so much in my life, and in ways that I never expected.

If I can offer my heart, my hand, my shoulder, and my love in half the measure that it has been offered to me, I can trust that I live an amazing, abundant life. It's not perfect, but the foundation is strong. I want nothing more than for you to feel that, too.

A Full-Circle Lesson Regarding the Path of Service

Moving back to Colorado was a pivotal time in my life and recovery. My role as a granddaughter was always deeply important, and I knew that my grandmother would have wanted me to be a part of my family at home. So, I leaned into them. I gained a great deal of pride in being a better daughter, a better sister, a cool aunt, and my most cherished role of all, mother. As the generations transitioned and my siblings, cousins, and I grew older, there was less family conflict. It wasn't absent, but it was much less than in my earlier life. I was truly grateful for the support and care my children received, especially when I had to work or attend a service committee meeting.

One night in September of 2000, when the girls were five and ten years old, I had a committee meeting, so Lorri watched them for me. I went to pick them up from her place at around nine p.m. It was a school night, and when I got there to pick them up, we were all three very tired and cranky. I was wearing myself out. I was wearing them out, too. While I felt like I was contributing in a significant way to AA, to my career, and to the livelihood that supported our little trio, I saw my small children sleeping in the car as I parked in the garage. I felt so bad that I had had to wake them. They hadn't been tucked in or brushed their teeth. There was no bedtime story. They were sleeping in the car because of my busy life, and I had to disrupt their sleep to get them inside.

I woke a very sleepy Angel, who protested, "Just let me sleep in the car." She was not very happy. She slowly walked in, and I carried Rae into the house. I had a very clear insight that I was repeating a pattern from my childhood conditioning. It wasn't really an epiphany, just a moment of realization that I was not present enough for my own children.

So, I resigned from every service commitment outside of my home, literally, the next day.

It was a moment of guilt and gift. A couple of years into more fully and consistently working the program, I realized that I had a misconception that my service work needed to be predominantly based in my volunteer commitments to AA, but the time I was devoting to having two to four jobs and maintaining the message of AA was taking away from the time my children needed and deserved. I had always been extremely proud and honored to say that my children have never seen me drunk. However, my children weren't seeing me enough in general.

I was grateful for the realization, as I'd been shuffling far too much, and my girls deserved more of that side of my capabilities—the side of me that could mitigate conflict in a committee needed to be present for the arguments between siblings. The side of me that was so creative with solutions needed to be innovative in how I invited my girls to cook or clean together. The side of me that was committed to serving and helping others needed to be a loving shoulder and guide when one of my own daughters had hurt feelings from a friend or a difficult moment at school. The gift was realizing my role at home was a more valued service than anywhere else in my life. The guilt was that I didn't recognize it sooner.

While I still had more than one job to pay the bills and they weren't raised in the same home since birth, I was more present, and I provided a far more stable life than the one I had known as a child. I was engaged and never missed a school play, awards ceremony, sporting event, or parent-teacher conference. Both of my girls had good attendance and decent grades. They not only knew that I was there, but also that I *wanted* to be there, and that I truly loved them.

I have to humbly admit that managing a heavy load of service both with my profession and my personal life is still something I struggle to balance, but family remains a priority over all other things.

A Full-Circle Reflection of Motherhood

My girls and I often prayed together. Sometimes, at bedtime or in the car, but my favorite moments were when one or both of them would join me in me in the mornings for my daily committed ritual.

A deeply imprinted memory was of a cold, snowy morning. We had enough snow that it was a snow day! Most of the city had called in and schools were closed. The girls and I were all stoked that we had the day at home together. I was sitting in my prayer chair under a blanket with my coffee steaming on the end table, and Angel came down and sat by me. Rae often slept with Angel or me, so she wasn't far behind. We were snuggled closely in the big chair, giving thanks for the things we felt grateful for, as well as praying for all those we wanted to bless on that day. I opened my eyes and looked at my sweet daughters with their eyes closed and their hearts so willing to give blessings, and it hit me. I had this beautiful full-circle moment of true realization that I had done it—I'd broken the chains. The richness of that connected moment was powerful.

My children had a sacred space for a home, and they were safe. It wasn't perfect, but to use the phrase I shared about my childhood in relevance to raising my children, it was below-average dysfunction. There wasn't a father present, but I held my own as mom and dad. The bills were paid. They were in good schools, surrounded by good friends and supportive parents, and they had only known the version of me that is a woman of integrity, principle, and intention to truly do right by them in every way I could. They never once questioned how loved or important they were. They knew.

The elation in that realization brought tears to my eyes. As it did, both of them noticed and became very concerned. "What's wrong, Mom?" Angel said.

"Absolutely nothing. This is the most perfect moment of my life. These are tears of joy, my beauty. I am just so happy to be your mama." And we snuggled closer, and they truly understood. It is a moment I'll always remember.

Providing a home for my children that was stable, comfortable, and filled with love and connection is something I cherish. It is proof of generational healing.

A Full-Circle Walk of Purpose

In the last few years of my career in the staffing industry, I was often overheard discussing spirituality and metaphysics with clients and candidates whom we were placing. I had a reputation for pushing the boundaries of what was considered professional and what I regarded as merely compassionate and supportive. At one point, a manager, who was also a good friend, Joline, questioned my professionalism because I had incorporated spirituality into many conversations with unemployed candidates, as I felt compelled to support them in that way. It led to many discussions with her about the tie between our professional life and livelihood, and the incorporation of spirit. We were in a field that, by general standards, had nothing to do with spirituality. However, it was a part of me that I simply could not help but apply to all areas of my life.

I took pride in a progressive career in the staffing industry, including the compassion I showed to all those I connected with. I received several promotions and awards and gained more stature than I'd ever anticipated when I started back in 1992. Unfortunately, with each promotion and the gain of greater authority came disheartening insights into the deeper workings of Corporate America. I could no longer reconcile my professional walk with my spiritual growth.

I was in my late thirties at the time of my "mid-life awakening."

During my daily quiet time prayers, I began to ask God for signs as to where I needed to be. My soul knew it was time for a change, so I just relied on the Divine to show me the way.

I had had many amazing signs in my life that the Divine was protecting and guiding me. My level of trust in change for the better was significantly stronger. I knew I needed to make a move that would both provide for my own family but also honor a deeper calling of my soul to serve in the name of healing and divinity.

I was struggling with weight loss at the time, too. So, in August of 2006, I went to see a hypnotherapist to address it. I had no intention of discussing career change. However, in my initial consultation with Debra Berndt-Maldonado, a true gift to the world in so many ways, I knew this would be my new career. Just sitting with her and learning how she'd left Corporate America for this field, and the nature of how profoundly she'd helped people with various issues, from weight loss to trauma, or in the arena of performance and sleep, I knew right away that this was why I'd *really* come to see her.

I had helped people with the path of recovery for many years, and my desire to expand the way I served was strong. That first meeting felt like a ton of bricks had landed on the ground before me, laying a golden path.

This was in just that first conversation! I hadn't even had an actual hypnotherapy session yet.

The snowball effect from that meeting was profound. The training program I selected was set to begin in just a few short months, in February of 2007. It was at a local school, and all classes were held on weekends throughout 2007 and into early 2008. In early 2007, I received a substantial bonus that covered all of my tuition in full.

At the time, Rae and I had both been training in martial arts, and I tore my left ACL. My surgery to reconstruct it was in March of 2007, and while in physical therapy, the owner of the PT facility learned that I was training to become a hypnotherapist and agreed to be one of my practice clients. I was seeing numerous practice clients for free during the training, and he had a small office in the facility that we used. He allowed me to use this space for my sessions with him and many others over the course of two years. Yes, TWO YEARS of free office space!

The most remarkable moment of synchronicity in this career change was the call I received five minutes after submitting my resignation letter in February 2008. I was still completing some of my specialty courses in metaphysical hypnotherapy but had passed all of my initial exams in late 2007, becoming officially certified as an International Hypnotherapist. I'd been formally seeing hypnotherapy clients for a few months and was ready to make the complete transition to becoming a business owner. I was nervous, but ready.

I hit send on my resignation email and sat at my desk, a little overwhelmed with both elation and fear. I was ending a sixteen-year career and taking a leap of faith. I was nervous about financial security because I didn't have a strong enough practice to sustain myself. However, I was so burned out that I couldn't stay in my old career with any integrity, as I wasn't honoring the role well either.

Then my cell phone rang.

"Hello. This is Paula," is how I always answered.

"Oh my gosh, I can't believe I remembered your number by heart! How long has it been, a year?" said the familiar voice of my dear friend and former boss, Joline. Yes, the same Joline who questioned my professionalism because I was too spiritual.

"Hi, Jo! It's so nice to hear from you!"

"Well, you wouldn't believe it," she said, "but I'm all into the woo now, too!" She laughed. "I'm sure that is why I remembered your number out of the blue."

"Well, your timing is wild," I replied. "I just sent in my resignation letter. I'm leaving the industry."

"Wow! That is wild. Where are you going?"

"I just got certified as a hypnotherapist and have started my practice. I'm not fully up and running, but I never will be unless I give it a real go. How are you doing?"

"Well, actually, I'm calling to see if you know anyone who could come to work for me part-time as a consultant. I just started my own boutique staffing firm, and I just need someone with expertise to help out while I get my own business off the ground, too."

"I know someone who just resigned that could use a part-time transition gig," I laughed.

"Now I *really* know why I remembered your number!"

I worked for Joline for a little over a year, and we both built our businesses. That call is yet another one of those moments that strengthened my faith in the Divine and my inner connection as a whole. It is yet another example of how maintaining the four pillars of connection brought synchronicity and magic into my life.

There is a ton more to this beautiful profession that I love and have embraced since late 2007, but that is its own book for a later date. I have been able to provide for my children as a single mother since my divorce in 1998 and am in a career that I profoundly love and honor. I know that it is evolving, but this professional path is one that I am deeply grateful for and proud of.

Full-Circle Family Moments

Living back home and being in recovery, I witnessed my mother's growth as she interacted with the next generation, and it was quite beautiful. She still had some of the difficult aspects of her personality, such as health problems and a penchant for drama, but she grew in her capacity as a mother and grandmother once she married my stepfather, Don.

They were truly great together, even in their rough spots. She had a great love for bringing the family together. As a grandmother, her soul truly shined. Witnessing this second chance at motherhood for her as a grandmother is something I cherish. It was not only healing, but it brought a deeper connection to understanding her as a whole. She had matured a great deal and allowed herself to love and be loved in return, and her grandchildren were crazy about her.

We gathered as a family at least five times each year as my daughters were growing up. We had the holidays of Christmas, Thanksgiving, and Easter, but we also celebrated family birthdays for the seasons. Lorri and Jeff both had spouses and children, and Don's mother, sons and grandchildren often joined us. With family and often friends, there were about twenty people on any given occasion.

As with the family gatherings of my childhood, we would all arrive, hug one another, compliment one another on looks and how fast we thought the little one's new shoes would make them run, and just get the biggest glow watching the kids open gifts or go on one of the epic Easter egg hunts. The food was always amazing, and there was always too much. It was much of the same as what I had loved as a child. The difference was in how the gatherings unfolded.

There would often be these special moments of connection and sweet conversations about each other's lives. We sat together and talked, enjoying the transition from one chat to another. I was the only adult who was fully committed to no alcohol or other mind-altering substances, but there was never a full-blown excess moment. It was so different from how the gatherings of my youth always ended.

These gatherings were treasured, and it was rare that one of the family didn't make it. Even as the generations of Lorri's, Jeff's, and my children were getting older, we all still loved being together. The familial connection had some healing, too. There was a connection that could easily be likened to community.

I'll never know what to credit the family healing to for sure, and I don't think my mother ever fully understood the extent of my drinking and behavior. I never really wanted her to. But I know she was proud of my recovery. So, I'm not sure if that's part of why she held family gatherings, or if it was simply maturity. I just know, no matter the reason, I'm deeply grateful that it shifted as the generations grew up. The memories are priceless.

Full Circle with My Mother

I spent a great deal of my life being angry at my mother and resentful that she was not the perfect version of a mother I had wanted. As I did my own inner work, and especially as I became a mother, I gained not only an understanding of her but also a level of forgiveness that surpassed any other person I had been hurt by. She had been apologizing for my childhood for many years now, and I gained a deep sorrow for the guilt she carried. I saw her from a healthier set of eyes. I grew to fully accept her. All of the resentment fell away, and I became tuned into the person that she was, not the person that I'd wished she were.

As her health began to decline in 2015, I initially wanted to offer her every healing modality and hypnotherapy practice that I knew. She was polite about it, but not interested. I'd gained a great deal of knowledge about holistic healing and wanted to share that with her, but she was very accustomed to trusting what her medical doctors advised or suggested, typically prescription medications. I quickly learned that my insistence on her trying things I was researching and utilizing in the alternative health world both made her nervous and caused her a great deal of stress. So, I stepped back and just began supporting her in whatever path made her most comfortable. I accepted her as she was, and I accepted that her decline would likely be much faster than I wanted.

I grew to acknowledge and love the sweet side of her that had always been there. She would call and check in on me and my girls more than any other person in my life. She would quickly turn the conversation to the physical difficulty of the day, and rather than trying to offer a solution, I would simply tell her how sorry I was to hear it and ask if there was anything I could do. She typically said no as she just wanted to be loved and know that I cared. I would bring flowers and some essential oils, but that was the extent of it, offerings of beautiful sight and smell.

In 2020, at the beginning of the pandemic, she was nearing hospice care, and my stepfather found an at-home care provider to assist with medications, bathing, and housekeeping. At the same time, my work was virtually crippled by the many shutdowns around the country, so I was able to help. Then the care provider had some personal matters arise, so I stepped in and spent the last three weeks of her life as her primary at-home hospice provider. In coordination with actual hospice care providers who came once a day, I managed all of her medications, bathing, mobility, and most of all, her entertainment.

In moments while she was awake, I would watch a TV show with her or sing her favorite songs to her. She loved music by Elvis, Frank Sinatra, Patsy Cline, and even the Steve Miller Band. In her final days, she neither ate nor drank anything, not even water. I would put a few drops of water in her mouth to moisten her lips, but she was mostly catatonic. She didn't close her eyes for almost four days, and it was fascinating to see her just stare as if watching the heavens. She was very peaceful, yet very absent. Those moments are bittersweet. I was relieved that she wouldn't be suffering any longer, but I was deeply saddened that she never really lived peacefully or healthily. She was always troubled by various conflicts, worries, or stresses. And while I had sincerely wished for the experience of her in a stronger or healthier state, it was a beautiful experience to fully come to terms with who she was rather than who I'd wanted her to be.

On June 30, 2020, I was singing all the songs. I couldn't ever tell if she liked it or if it bothered her, but I was singing from a place of love. My stepdad came in and joined my little concert. We both sang a few of her favorites together, and then we were overwhelmed with emotion, knowing the end was near. So, we stepped out to sit in the sun and just catch our breath. When we returned a few minutes later, she was gone. Just like my grandmother, she didn't want to leave in front of us.

Being her hospice provider and walking her home over those few weeks was one of the most honorable things I've ever done. Had I not done my inner healing work, that would have never happened.

Full Circle on the Circle of Life

If there's anything that I know, it's that life has many full-circle moments and reflections in the grand scheme of things. As I've reflected on my life, over all of these pages, I could add a few more chapters about many of those I love and have shared about in this book. So, for the sake of simplicity, let me give you a few snapshots.

I'm still in touch with many of the friends that I made as a teen. We all grew up, and most are really sound, but not all. I remain closest to Lisa, Bonnie, and Cheri. In fact, Cheri and I just had dinner a few weeks ago in San Diego, where she lives now. She is healthy, beautiful, and we share many of the same spiritual views.

I remarried in 2024 to a wonderful man who is the best friend that I've ever had. Again, I could (and may) write an entire book about my journey to finding this kind of love. I have two amazing stepchildren who are in college and high school, and a beautiful family on his side that I love.

I talk to one or both of my daughters almost daily. As they've grown into beautiful and wise adult women, they have been real and honest about their own perspectives on their upbringing. I aced most of it and had some epic fails, but overall, I am deeply grateful that we are close.

Since my mother's passing, the family doesn't gather as much. Angel got married in 2016 and moved to Texas. My stepdad, Don, moved to Mexico and visits often. We make the best of what we can, and we reflect on the legacy of my mother's gift of unifying us as well as her capacity for forgiveness. I never saw it as clearly when I was younger, but her greatest trait was her ability to not only forgive but to take responsibility for her mistakes. I will forever be grateful for this example as I see it with such clarity today.

The full circle that I cherish the most is being a grandmother. Angel has two children, and when I visit Texas and stay in her guest room, my grandchildren light up when they see me. We have talks. We read. We go for walks, play, and giggle, and my granddaughter, the eldest, loves to help me cook in their kitchen.

The most beautiful moments are the ones when my granddaughter comes into the room where I sleep at bedtime. She curls up facing me, and we have a little talk before we sleep. She holds my hand and knows that she is absolutely cherished. I am a grandmother, and there's a little girl who knows she's safe, loved, and secure by my side.

ABOUT THE AUTHOR

Paula Robbins is a metaphysical hypnotherapist, coach, speaker, and author who has spent more than thirty years helping people around the globe break free from the grip of trauma. She has guided hundreds of clients to release crippling anxiety and PTSD, reclaim empowerment, and live with peace, trust, and spiritual connection. Her work is grounded in both lived experience and professional expertise.

Having navigated her own journey through recovery and healing, Paula weaves together personal truth with practical tools, offering readers not just hope but a roadmap for lasting transformation.

When she isn't working, Paula is dedicated to her family, building strength of body, mind, and spirit, and finding joy in life's simplest moments. She lives her message: that even in the most difficult seasons, light can be found and trust restored.

Hitchhiking Into Recovery is the first book in Paula's Beautiful Ugly Lessons series, created to inspire readers to step into wholeness, freedom, and trust in themselves and life.

To stay in touch and learn more, visit PaulaRobbins.com.

For more great books from Empower Press
Visit Books.GracePointPublishing.com

EMPOWER
PRESS

If you enjoyed reading *Hitchhiking into Recovery* and purchased it through an online retailer, please return to the site and write a review to help others find the book.